No Magic Wand

No Magic Wand

The Idealization of Science in Law

David S. Caudill and Lewis H. LaRue

ROWMAN & LITTLEFIELD PUBLISHERS, INC.
Lanham • Boulder • New York • Toronto • Oxford

Published in cooperation with the Center for Public Justice

ROWMAN & LITTLEFIELD PUBLISHERS, INC.

Published in the United States of America
by Rowman & Littlefield Publishers, Inc.
A wholly owned subsidiary of The Rowman & Littlefield Publishing Group, Inc.
4501 Forbes Boulevard, Suite 200, Lanham, Maryland 20706
www.rowmanlittlefield.com

PO Box 317, Oxford
OX2 9RU, UK

Copyright © 2006 by Center for Public Justice
Published in cooperation with the Center for Public Justice.

British Library Cataloguing in Publication Information Available

Library of Congress Cataloging-in-Publication Data

Caudill, David Stanley.
  No magic wand : the idealization of science in law / David S. Caudill and Lewis H.
LaRue.
      p. cm.
  Includes bibliographical references and index.
  ISBN-13: 978-0-7425-5022-3 (cloth : alk. paper)
  ISBN-10: 0-7425-5022-2 (cloth : alk. paper)
  ISBN-13: 978-0-7425-5023-0 (pbk. : alk. paper)
  ISBN-10: 0-7425-5023-0 (pbk. : alk. paper)
  1. Evidence, Expert. 2. Forensic sciences. 3. Science and law. 4. Judicial process. I.
LaRue, Lewis H. II. Title.
K5485.C38 2006
363.25—dc22   2006005566

Printed in the United States of America

♾™ The paper used in this publication meets the minimum requirements of American
National Standard for Information Sciences—Permanence of Paper for Printed Library
Materials, ANSI/NISO Z39.48-1992.

For Penny and Sue . . .

Contents

Acknowledgments

The material for this book originated in (i) several conference papers delivered at the annual meetings of the Society for the Sociological Study of Science, the Southeastern Association of Law Schools, and the Society for Literature, Science and the Arts; (ii) two faculty colloquia at Villanova University School of Law; and (iii) numerous publications in law journals. Chapters 1–4 include substantial revisions of the following articles that we coauthored: "Post-*Trilogy* Science in the Courtroom: What Are the Judges Doing?" 13 *Journal of Civil Litigation* 341–57 (Winter 2001–2002); "Post-*Trilogy* Science in the Courtroom, Part II: What Are the Judges *Still* Doing?" 15 *Journal of Civil Litigation* 1–14 (Spring 2003); "Why Judges Applying the *Daubert* Trilogy Need to Know about the Social, Institutional, and Rhetorical—and Not Just the Methodological—Aspects of Science," 45 *Boston College Law Review* 1–53 (December 2003); and "A Non-Romantic View of Expert Testimony," 35 *Seton Hall Law Review* 1–45 (2004). Chapters 5–6 include substantial revisions of the following articles by Professor Caudill: "Ethnography and the Idealized Accounts of Science in Law," 39 *San Diego Law Review* 269–305 (Spring 2002); "Law, Science, and Science Studies: Contrasting the Deposition of a Scientific Expert with Ethnographic Studies of Scientific Practice," 12 *Southern California Interdisciplinary Law Journal* 85–100 (2002); "Advocacy, Witnesses, and the Limits of Scientific Knowledge: Is There an Ethical Duty to Evaluate Your Expert's Testimony?" 39 *Idaho Law Review* 341–55 (2003); and "*Sociotechnical* Arguments in Scientific Discourse: Expert Depositions in Tobacco Litigation," 24 *Review of Litigation* 1–56 (Winter 2005).

We are grateful to a host of colleagues and friends at our own law schools—at Villanova University and Washington and Lee University—and elsewhere in the academy for their encouragement and criticism. David

Caudill would especially like to thank Dean David Partlett, Dean Mark Sargent, and Professors Gary Edmond, Richard Redding, Barbara Allen, David Mercer, Joseph Ulrich, Michael Lynch, Simon Cole, Hugh Crawford, Peter Goodrich, and Costas Douzinas. Lewis LaRue thanks John Maguire, who first taught him evidence; Clyde Mann, in whose court he had to learn to present evidence correctly; and, David Shun, who taught him how to rethink everything. Debts are owed to many, but the most is owed to these three people.

We are also grateful to Vera Mencer and Sally Wieringa for their help in preparing the manuscript for the publisher. Finally, we wish to thank Jim Skillen, president of the Center for Public Justice, and Rowman and Littlefield editors Chris Anzalone and Lea Gift for bringing our book to print.

Foreword

David Caudill and Lewis LaRue argue in this book that "we should not imagine that science is a magic wand that with one wave can solve all social problems; to do so is to idealize." Their concern is with the inappropriate or questionable outcomes of court cases in which judges and lawyers idealize science, either by crediting too strongly the testimony of all scientific experts, or by discrediting the testimony of scientists who concede their limitations. As the authors also show, much the same idealization of science is at work in legislative and administrative settings where an appeal to scientific evidence is supposed to settle a matter or is judged to be insufficient to settle a matter.

Scientific authority has become ever more important in the shaping of society and the law over the past two centuries. Yet the authority of science does not stand alone; it is part of a larger range of contending authorities in contemporary society. The question then is how science should be evaluated, and how its claims should be treated by other authorities such as judges in courtrooms, legislators in Congress, and educators in schools, colleges, and the law schools themselves. This is one of the most contentious and critical questions of our day because concerns about health and safety, for example, loom ever larger in all spheres of life.

Therefore, anyone who has an interest in public justice—in the soundness of our political order under law—will find this book to be of great value. Whether one is most concerned about the high cost of some jury awards in medical malpractice cases or about Congress's handling of scientific evidence on global warming or the health risks of smoking, this book illuminates the landscape. The authors aim primarily to assess disputes over the use of scientific evidence in the courtroom and in the arena of legal scholarship, but they do their work in a way that opens up wide vistas on the meaning of sci-entific authority and how legal and governmental authorities should deal with it. This is creative analysis and constructive legal argument at its best.

James W. Skillen, President
Center for Public Justice

Introduction

Our focus in this book is on the current use of science in the courtroom. One should not underestimate the importance of this topic—some estimate that 75 percent of disputed civil cases involve one or more expert witnesses (who testify to the relevance of science to the case before the court), and that within that 75 percent, the median number of witnesses is four. Of course, merely because lawyers and judges see scientific experts daily does not mean that they understand accurately what these experts are saying. Indeed, they regularly experience problems, and some are baffled at how to use scientific testimony to help argue or decide cases. Moreover, a new problem has developed: the United States Supreme Court declared in 1993 that federal courts should not admit expert testimony unless the gatekeeping judge is satisfied that the content of the testimony is "reliable"; and supreme courts of many states have followed the lead of our nation's highest court (even though they are not technically required to do so). As we will explain in due course, *reliability* is a term of art in law, but this new standard of reliability has generated some obvious problems for our nation's judiciary. How are judges, and the lawyers who argue before them, to decide whether a scientist is presenting reliable or unreliable evidence? Judges and lawyers have stumbled into debating the very question that those who study the history, philosophy, and sociology of science have been debating: What is good science? Anyone with more than a passing interest in that question will find it profitable to compare what is happening in today's courts with traditional and contemporary studies of scientific knowledge.

We imagine (and hope) that those who might have more than a passing interest in our book will include scholars in political science, economics, and public administration who study and teach the process of making public policy. Such scholars often investigate and criticize how science is used in making policy, and we believe they will be interested in how science is used in deciding cases. Historians and sociologists study how science itself gets made, and we believe that they will also be intrigued by the fact that their core question—How is science made?—routinely becomes an issue in court. Finally, our colleagues in the legal academy who teach scientific evidence will be interested, but we do wish to caution them that we have written for a non-legal audience, and that we have not observed the conventions of law review prose, which we confess freely, believing this to be a virtue, not a vice.

Although there are many books about the relevance of science to law and policy, this book is different from most law-and-science books. Rather than focusing on the legislative or administrative process, and on how science is used to set policy, we look at the adjudicative context, the courtroom. Although adjudication is quite different from the legislative or administrative context, many of the problems concerning the best way to use science are the same. For example, those who write regulations or statutes (in the administrative or legislative arenas) always look to the future, while trial lawyers and judges look to the past. Nevertheless, legislators and administrators are provoked to consider changes for the future because of troubles that have arisen in the past, and judges do worry about the consequences of their decisions and the community's response. The distinction between the two contexts remains valid, however, especially when incentives in the policy context and in litigation are contrasted. Administrators and legislators hope to change the world in accordance with their agendas, but litigators and judges have simpler motives: to win, or to decide, a case. Consider mass tort litigation, such as that exemplified by the Dalkon Shield contraceptive or the Bendectin antinausea drug cases: the lawyers for the plaintiffs in such cases want lots of money to compensate the victims for their injuries (and the lawyers for their time), while the defense lawyers want to limit their clients' losses *in the specific case at issue*. Such cases will have enormous policy consequences, yet the primary and immediate incentives are more crude.

That said, note that the very same scientific enterprise is at work in both the policy and litigation contexts. We began this study with the presumption that the problems of science in the courtroom would be strikingly different from the problems of science in the policy context, yet in the end we found more common ground than we imagined. The goal of making decisions on the basis of reliable scientific evidence—whether concerning risk of a new drug or liability for an old drug—is the same. Consequently, we are confident that this book will be relevant both to those who study the judicial process as well as to those who study administrative or legislative processes.

The problem we identify in law, with respect to science, is one of idealization. Many judges and lawyers look to science to provide stability—the answer!—to a legal controversy. Knowing that law is a cultural institution characterized by advocacy and rhetoric, such judges and lawyers often imagine that science is better than that—it should stand, they think, above culture, advocacy, and rhetoric. In our view, however, science is a pragmatic enterprise, with practical and local goals and limitations. Science is not only rigorous and methodological, it also betrays inevitable social, rhetorical, and institutional interests and aspects; these latter features of science are therefore not always markers of bad science, but are also characteristics of the best science. It is not a critique of a useful scientific theory to identify the ambitions, interests, funding, persuasive models, and credentials that preceded *and even maintain* its acceptance in the scientific community. We call this a non-romantic view of science to distinguish it from the view of those who see science at its best as an enterprise that transcends social interests, politics, rhetoric, debate, history, and other human aspects. As we will show, trial judges who have a romantic view of science tend, alternatively, to make two mistakes: sometimes they disallow good science because the scientific expert does not live up to their idealistic image of science; and paradoxically, sometimes they allow bad science on the basis of its social authority alone. In both cases, a failure to understand the practical goals and limitations of science leads to the phenomenon of a distinctively "legal" science in the courtroom that does not match the reality in which scientists work. In response, some scholars confirm their own idealization of science by blaming judges for being scientifically unsophisticated, juries for being scientifically illiterate, and lawyers for being scientifically dishonest. Other scholars begin to idealize the law, believing that surely an educated gatekeeping judge, an objective jury, or an honest attorney can ensure that reliable science is determinative in a trial. In our view, one must maintain a non-romantic vision of both science and law, for both are cultural enterprises that rely, for example, not only on logic and methodology, but also on social conventions, rhetorical moves, and institutional credentializing. Indeed, we demonstrate that thesis both by conducting interviews with scientists and by analyzing several deposition transcripts from recent tobacco litigation. The discourse of scientists themselves, and of the lawyers who depose them, betrays an unwitting reliance on arguments based on social, historical, and institutional frameworks, in addition to their technical arguments.

Recent work in science studies—variously referred to as "science-and-technology studies" or the "sociology of scientific knowledge"—has confirmed that the polarization between utter faith and confidence in science, on the one hand, and criticism of science as a social construction, on the other, is unnecessary. Science is a product of *both* (i) observation and experiment, with respect to natural reality, *and* (ii) norms, conventions, and expectations within the scientific community. In legal literature, however, the notion persists that an expert with "biases, interests, and motivations" is thereby discredited, as if such aspects of humanity are always bad (they aren't), and as if good scientists are never biased toward a favored theory (they are), never interested in some problems and not others (they are), and never motivated toward economic success (they are). Our purpose is to argue for an appropriately modest view of scientific expertise and legal processes, and to show how such views can assist judges and lawyers, and potentially administrators and legislators, in recognizing and appropriating the best science in law.

The sequence of topics is straightforward. We will begin with discussing what happens at trials, with a focus on the interplay between trial courts and the appellate courts that supervise them. Next we move away from the courtroom into the legal academy, and we give a highly abbreviated summary of what legal academics have said about what the judges are doing. Then we move to a less-formal arena, the interaction of lawyers and scientists outside the courtroom in the pretrial investigation of claims, which we compare to ethnographic studies of scientists in their laboratories. We end by comparing what we have done with a few examples from the sociology of science, the history of science, and science in legislation.

Chapter One

What's the Problem?

THE IDEALIZATION OF SCIENCE IN LAW

[M]any of the luminaries of physics, from Bohr and Heisenberg on down, took the radical step of denying the existence of an independently existing physical world altogether, and, surprisingly, got away with it. In other, i.e., nonscientific, contexts, the difference between those who are committed to an independently existing reality and those who are not is roughly correlated with the distinction between the sane and the psychotic.[1]

In Rebecca Goldstein's popular novel about quantum physicists, her protagonist Justin Childs is enraged by the "nonsense . . . that *measurement creates reality so that it is simply meaningless to ask what's going on when no measurement is taking place*." Later in the story, however, he learns (from his mentor, who failed in his objectivist challenge to Bohr and Heisenberg) something about the way science works:

[T]he last thing in the world I ever expected was to be ignored. . . . I thought that it was only the objective merits of the work itself that mattered, especially in science. If not in science, then where else? . . . I didn't know how things really work . . . , how it gets decided what should be paid attention to . . . . The big shots decide and the little shots just march lock-stepped into line.[2]

This brief literary representation captures what is going on nowadays in the so-called science wars[3]: on one side are the believers in science as an enterprise that reports on natural reality, or at least successfully represents nature with models that correspond to reality; on the other side are those who view science as a social, rhetorical, and institutional enterprise that only manages to convince us that it deals in natural reality. Because the latter position—that

1

reality is constructed (not discovered) by scientists—is so counterintuitive, it sounds nonsensical, almost psychotic, to believers in science. And yet, if the social, institutional, and rhetorical structures of the scientific enterprise, rather than "nature," effectively determine what "gets . . . paid attention to," then reality as we know it *is* to some extent constructed.

Does this academic debate among philosophers, historians, and sociologists of science really matter? After all, science progresses without regard to the science wars, and scientists are likely oblivious to the concerns of social constructivists, who do not seem to be providing useful insights to the scientific enterprise. We will argue, however, that the science wars are significant for law because the issues raised in this debate provide insights as to what trial judges need to know about science to carry out their gatekeeping role with respect to proffered expert testimony. Moreover, the position a judge takes, perhaps unwittingly, with respect to the status and authority of science, actually matters—cases are often won or lost on the basis of scientific evidence, and appeals are so costly that a trial judge's understanding of science is often determinative.

Given the privileged position of science in law as a stabilizer of legal disputes, one might assume that the courtroom is closely aligned (with respect to the science wars) with the believers in science. Indeed, some commentators have suggested that in the wake of three recent U.S. Supreme Court opinions (known as the *Daubert* Trilogy),[4] "legal culture must assimilate the scientific culture."[5] Law professor Michael Saks has even suggested that admissibility decisions as to most scientific evidence should be treated as matters of law because the facts of science have "quite a trans-case and law-like nature."[6] Such comments suggest that expertise is grounded in *reality*, and is decidedly *not* a matter of rhetoric or social construction. Courts should therefore, from this vantage, defer to science. On the other hand, some commentators suggest that science is just another cultural activity, like law, such that deference is not appropriate;[7] from this vantage, the law can and should construct its own legal "science," which need not be considered inferior, because mainstream science is also a construction. In a similar formulation, some argue that scientific knowledge is "reconstructed and framed" in court, where the scientific method is a "representational device" like other "normative images" (e.g., general acceptance, or peer review and publication), which "are better understood as *ex post facto* explanations and a professional rhetoric."[8] The science wars, it appears, have arrived in legal discourse.

In our view, the science wars present a false dichotomy to which the law should not submit. Believers in science idealize the scientific enterprise to such a degree that the inevitable social, institutional, and rhetorical aspects of science—its pragmatic features—are neither acknowledged nor discussed.

Legal commentary on the *Daubert* Trilogy is dominated by such idealization,[9] thereby marginalizing social studies of science in legal scholarship.[10] Oddly however, while social constructivists do not idealize science, they *do* idealize the social aspects of science to a degree that the successes of science are either ignored or eclipsed. Neither option is particularly attractive, which leads many philosophers and social analysts to conclude that science is *both* productive of knowledge about the world *and* a social, institutional, and rhetorical enterprise. Historically,

> Western science derives from an earlier art of *rhetoric*, chronologically (i.e., with regard to the sequence of developments in our tradition), as well as systematically (regarding the nature of scientific activity). Paul Feyerabend goes as far as declaring that *propaganda* belongs to the essence of science, a view also held, but less outrageously formulated, by T. S. Kuhn in his theory of scientific paradigms. Far from dismissing science as mere rhetoric—a hopeless attempt in view of its practical and technological triumphs—this position states the obvious fact that all sciences, including the most abstract and mathematized disciplines, are social endeavors which must be carried out through the channels and means, and according to the rules, of communication available to a community of practitioners.[11]

That perspective does not represent either extreme in the science wars—it does not idealize either science or social determinants. Surprisingly, recent fieldwork in the public understanding of science confirms that

> [l]ay attitudes toward science, technology and other esoteric forms of expertise . . . tend to express the same mixed attitudes of reverence and reserve, approval and disquiet, enthusiasm and antipathy, which [many] philosophers and social analysts . . . express in their writings.[12]

Even more surprising than the fact that the public's reaction to science is mixed is our finding that many appellate judges (who review cases on appeal from a trial court) are just like the public: they are (i) more willing to view science as an enterprise with local and practical goals and limitations, and therefore are (ii) less willing to idealize or defer to science than the believers in science (in the science wars) are, but at the same time are (iii) nevertheless willing to appropriate science, as a pragmatic enterprise, when it is a reliable producer of useful knowledge.

Too many trial judges, however, idealize science. The paradoxical consequence of idealizing science is that such trial judges are either too harsh or too generous toward scientific experts in the courtroom. By "too harsh," we mean that such a trial judge sometimes expects too much from science, which after all is not a perfect enterprise. By "too generous," we mean that such a trial judge sometimes idolizes scientific authority without critically evaluating its limitations. In either case, the best science for a particular lawsuit can be missed. Our response is to describe a pragmatic, realistic, and non-romantic view of science that recognizes its goals and limitations. While it is commonplace to criticize judges for having a deficient understanding of scientific methodology, we hope to show that judges need to appreciate the social—and not just the methodological—aspects of science. Indeed, in many of the appellate opinions we analyze in this book, trial judges have erred in more subtle and interesting ways than merely by misunderstanding methodology.

Our recurring reference to the social, institutional, and rhetorical features of science, as opposed to its methodological features, merits a preliminary explanation. Social aspects of science include its communal, rather than individualistic, structures such as historical background, experimental conventions, shared standards of legitimacy, negotiation, consensus building, and the notion of an audience that evaluates the production of knowledge. Science's institutional features, which are also social, include training, credentializing, and gatekeeping by way of granting degrees, positions, funding, or publicity. The rhetorical features of science include its narrative and textual aspects such as techniques of persuasion, use of metaphors, and linguistic conventions. While these factors often fade into the background when judges focus on methodological features such as testing or rates of error, there is no reason to assume that they are dispensable or insignificant in the final, that is, the *methodological*, analysis. Indeed, methodology itself relies on social, institutional, and rhetorical conventions; our current canons for how scientists should do their work are the product of history, and there is no reason to believe that we have reached end-time in their evolution. Significantly however, there is no reason to assume that simply because of these social features, nature or reality has nothing to do with scientific knowledge. On the other hand, the understandable sense that one must choose between a social explanation and a natural explanation for scientific progress, which we deem a false dualism, helps explain why the social aspects of science are often not discussed in *Daubert* Trilogy jurisprudence.

THE LEGAL CONTEXT

The use of science in lawsuits is not new, but we will not review history. Instead, we will plunge into the current state of the law, which has been set by the three cases that we refer to as the *Daubert* Trilogy. The first case is *Daubert v. Merrell Dow Pharmaceuticals*,[13] which represented a sea change in the law of evidence and therefore generated an enormous amount of commentary. The case involved a birth-defect claim for damages against the manufacturer of the antinausea drug Bendectin, but by the time it arrived at the Supreme Court, it had evolved into a dispute over how to construe the Federal Rules of Evidence, and in particular, Rule 702, which purports to prescribe the rules for the admission of expert evidence into the trial courts of the federal system. Reading rules is generally a tedious task, but in this case the rule is blessedly brief, so we take the liberty of actually quoting the full text:

> If scientific, technical, or other specialized knowledge will assist the trier of fact to understand the evidence or to determine a fact in issue, a witness qualified as an expert by knowledge, skill, experience, training, or education, may testify thereto in the form of an opinion or otherwise.

As short as the passage is, not all of it was pertinent to the dispute. Indeed, the dispute before the Court centered on the following words: "If scientific . . . knowledge will assist the trier of fact . . . a witness qualified as an expert . . . may testify . . . ." Note that the rule is not limited to scientific experts—your local mechanic, though not a scientist, can testify as an expert on how an automobile ought to be repaired. However, in the *Daubert* case, the witnesses were in fact scientists, and so the court focused on the language that we have just quoted.

The significance of *Daubert* is that the Supreme Court read Rule 702 as imposing a duty on trial judges that came as a surprise to many commentators. Historically, judges deferred to general consensus in the scientific community. Yet according to the Court, the rule requires that trial judges make a preliminary finding before an expert witness can testify; in particular, if the witness claims to be a scientist, then the trial judge must determine whether the testimony is indeed based on "scientific . . . knowledge." Needless to say, the opinion imposes upon trial judges a daunting task, and in order to give some guidance, Justice Harry Blackmun's opinion offered some guidelines, though these turned out to be extremely controversial. (By the way, Blackmun did not attempt to apply his own guidelines to the facts of the case; he sent the case back to the lower courts to do this difficult task.) The first matter of controversy was over the exact meaning of the guidelines. What sort of instruction was Blackmun giving to trial judges? And the second matter of controversy was over the wisdom of these guidelines. Were the instructions sensible? Since Blackmun's words turned out to be highly controversial, we shall quote them with only some light editing. (We eliminate some procedural comments that are not pertinent to our discussion, but we include Justice Blackmun's citations, since we believe that those who read this book may be interested in knowing which sources Blackmun considered authoritative.)

Faced with a proffer of expert scientific testimony, then, the trial judge must determine at the outset whether the expert is proposing to testify to (1) scientific knowledge that (2) will assist the trier of fact to understand or determine a fact in issue. This entails a preliminary assessment of whether the reasoning or methodology underlying the testimony is scientifically valid and of whether that reasoning or methodology properly can be applied to the facts in issue. We are confident that federal judges possess the capacity to undertake this review. Many factors will bear on the inquiry, and we do not presume to set out a definitive checklist or test. But some general observations are appropriate.

Ordinarily, a key question to be answered in determining whether a theory or technique is scientific knowledge that will assist the trier of fact will be whether it can be (and has been) tested. "Scientific methodology today is based on generating hypotheses and testing them to see if they can be falsified; indeed, this methodology is what distinguishes science from other fields of human inquiry." Green ["Expert Witnesses and Sufficiency of Evidence in Toxic Substances Litigation: The Legacy of *Agent Orange* and Bendectin Litigation," 86 *Nw. U. L. Rev.* 643,] 645 [(1992)]. See also C. Hempel, Philosophy of Natural Science 49 (1966) ("The statements constituting a scientific explanation must be capable of empirical test"); K. Popper, Conjectures and Refutations: The Growth of Scientific Knowledge 37 (5th ed. 1989) ("The criterion of the scientific status of a theory is its falsifiability, or refutability, or testability") (emphasis deleted).

Another pertinent consideration is whether the theory or technique has been subjected to peer review and publication. Publication (which is but one element of peer review) is not a *sine qua non* of admissibility; it does not necessarily correlate with reliability, see S. Jasanoff, The Fifth Branch: Science Advisors as Policymakers 61–76 (1990), and in some instances well-grounded but innovative theories will not have been published, see Horrobin, The Philosophical Basis of Peer Review and the Suppression of Innovation, 263 *JAMA* 1438 (1990). Some propositions, moreover, are too particular, too new, or of too limited interest to be published. But submission to the scrutiny of the scientific community is a component of "good science," in part because it increases the likelihood that substantive flaws in methodology will be detected. See J. Ziman, Reliable Knowledge: An Exploration of the Grounds for Belief in Science 130–133 (1978); Relman & Angell, How Good Is Peer Review? 321 *New Eng. J. Med.* 827 (1989). The fact of publication (or lack thereof) in a peer reviewed journal thus will be a relevant, though not dispositive, consideration in assessing the scientific validity of a particular technique or methodology on which an opinion is premised.

Additionally, in the case of a particular scientific technique, the court ordinarily should consider the known or potential rate of error, see, e.g., *United States v. Smith*, 869 F.2d 348, 353–354 (CA7 1989) (surveying studies of the error rate of spectrographic voice identification technique), and the existence and maintenance of standards controlling the technique's operation, see *United States v. Williams*, 583 F.2d 1194, 1198 (CA2 1978) (noting professional organization's standard governing spectrographic analysis), cert. denied, 439 U.S. 1117, 59 L. Ed. 2d 77, 99 S. Ct. 1025 (1979).

Finally, "general acceptance" can yet have a bearing on the inquiry. A "reliability assessment does not require, although it does permit, explicit identification of a relevant scientific community and an express determination of a particular degree of acceptance within that community." *United States v. Downing*, 753 F.2d at 1238. See also 3 Weinstein & Berger para. 702[03], pp. 702–41 to 702–42. Widespread acceptance can be an important factor in ruling particular evidence admissible, and "a known technique which has been able to attract only minimal support within the community," *Downing*, 753 F.2d at 1238, may properly be viewed with skepticism.

The inquiry envisioned by Rule 702 is, we emphasize, a flexible one. Its overarching subject is the scientific validity—and thus the evidentiary relevance and reliability—of the principles that underlie a proposed submission. The focus, of course, must be solely on principles and methodology, not on the conclusions that they generate.

Those who are not familiar with the ways of legal academia cannot possibly imagine the number of trees that were destroyed in glossing these six paragraphs. In retrospect, we can say that the principal error committed by most commentators was to give undue prominence to four of these six paragraphs (the second through the fifth of that which is quoted above); these four paragraphs became known as "the *Daubert* criteria"—testability, low error rate, peer-reviewed publication, and general acceptance—and enormous effort was spent discussing them and debating their wisdom. In effect, for most legal scholars, the four factors became *the* four characteristics of science, thereby eclipsing discussion of other characteristics of science and establishing an idealized image of science. However, these commentators (we now rest on the wisdom of hindsight) ignored the caveats that preceded and followed these paragraphs; by giving undue emphasis to the actual wording of the four criteria, commentators were mislead into believing that the duty the Supreme Court imposed on trial judges was more regimented than it would turn out to be.

So let us return to Justice Blackmun's guidelines and give emphasis to his caveats. The last two sentences of the first paragraph, and the beginning of the second, read as follows:

> Many factors will bear on the inquiry, and we do not presume to set out a definitive checklist or test. But some general observations are appropriate.
>
> Ordinarily, [and here begins the listing of the four factors, starting with testability].[14]

We think that this language is important. Take it in reverse order. Consider the word "Ordinarily." The most plausible meaning of the word is that the factors apply in some, but not all, cases. The word "Ordinarily" begins the paragraph that discusses testability, and so in context, one can read this first factor (or the four as a group) as dispensable in some cases. Consider also the phrase, "general observations." Are we to discern the meaning of this sentence by contrasting *general* with *specific*? A plausible reading is that Blackmun means to establish general principles as distinguished from specific rules, and yet some commentators tended to treat the criterion of testability (and the four criteria as a group) as though such criteria were a set of specific rules that trial judges must administer.

Finally, note carefully the first sentence quoted above. We are told that "Many factors" will bear on the determination that there is valid science that was properly applied. Furthermore, we are told that the list of four factors that follow is not "a definitive checklist or test."[15] We find it hard to imagine how Justice Blackmun could have sent a clearer signal that one should not focus obsessively on the list of four factors. And one may recall that after the four factors were listed, Blackmun returned to this theme by reiterating that the "inquiry . . . is a flexible one."[16] Given all of this, no one should complain that the four factors are not specific or precise. Of course they are not, which is precisely what Blackmun intended.

We do not wish to be ill-tempered in this complaint, since in academic legal commentary it is customary practice to take language from a judicial opinion and treat it as though it were intended to be definitive. Many of these articles proceed hypothetically: *If* one takes the language quite literally, *then* what would the consequences be? Such a hypothetical inquiry can have considerable value, although it runs the risk of becoming irrelevant. Judges regularly refuse to be tied down by their own words. They retroactively reinterpret what they have said so as to avoid inconvenient consequences. One cannot wish away inconvenient language in a statute, but judges do wish away the words that they themselves have written.

At any rate, however one reads Justice Blackmun's initial statement of the four factors, when one reads the entire *Daubert* Trilogy, it becomes clear that his caveats are in fact important. The next case in the trilogy involved an electrician, with lung cancer, seeking damages against the manufacturers of PCBs (polychlorinated biphenyls), electrical transformers, and dielectric fluid; but again, by the time it arrived at the Supreme Court, the case was transformed into a controversy over two assertions in Blackmun's opinion that seem to be inconsistent. Blackmun writes that the trial judge must "focus . . . solely on principles and methodology, not on . . . conclusions," and yet he also states that whether the "methodology properly can be applied to the facts in issue" is a matter that the judges must decide.[17] The first sentence recommends viewing science in the abstract without regard to the conclusion or application in a particular case; the second sentence requires that judges evaluate the application. We think that one can conclude only one thing: these two sentences do not go well together, although with ingenuity one could come up with a possible reconciliation.[18] So how is this apparent inconsistency to be resolved?

In *General Electric v. Joiner*,[19] the second case in the trilogy, the tension was resolved in favor of the "application" thesis. In this case, the trial judge put the emphasis on the statement that one must decide whether the expert is properly *applying* the scientific methodology and principles to the case at hand; on the basis of a doubtful application, the trial judge excluded the expert's testimony. The intermediate court of appeals reversed, putting emphasis on Justice Blackmun's "methodology, not . . . conclusions" language, and concluding that the trial judge should not have worried about the application. Either decision is reasonable, but only one can be right. In *Joiner*, Chief Justice William Rehnquist sided with the trial judge by stating that "conclusions and methodology are not entirely distinct from one another." This "not entirely" thesis was reinforced and given bite by the following sentence: "The court may conclude that there is simply too great an analytical gap between the data and the opinion proffered."[20]

One should note that the expert in *Joiner* did not use improper methodology, so the result in the case demonstrates that the focus by some scholars on methodology is too narrow a focus. The expert in *Joiner* based his opinion on laboratory animal studies and epidemiological studies. All of the judges who looked at the case agreed that this methodology meets the test of being scientific. Yet this was not the problem with the evidence in *Joiner*; the problem was the "analytical gap."[21] The action, we might say, was in the application (and not in abstract scientific theories, principles, or methodology).

Unfortunately, the true import of *Joiner* was less than clear to those who read it, since the procedural posture of the case was a peculiar one. The precise issue before the Supreme Court was whether the court of appeals had used the proper standard to review the district court's decision to exclude the expert. The court of appeals thought that it should review what the trial judge had done de novo, that is, they should ask whether the trial judge got it right.[22] The Supreme Court disagreed, saying that courts of appeals should follow the customary standard for reviewing evidentiary rulings, which is to use the abuse-of-discretion standard, that is, they should ask whether the trial judge is "in the ball park."[23] Consequently, lawyers were puzzled by how seriously one should take the *Joiner* opinion.

That puzzle disappeared when the third case in the trilogy was decided. *Kumho Tire Co., Ltd. v. Carmichael*[24] establishes that one must take the *Joiner* case very seriously indeed, and the overall consequence is that one must give equal emphasis to all three cases in the trilogy if one is to understand the law. We can start by noting that *Kumho Tire* begins by declaring that the issue on which many commentators had focused in their glossing of the four factors, that is, "What is the difference between science and nonscience?" would often be unimportant for judging the admissibility of expert testimony.[25] The trial judge must subject all experts, whether they be scientific or not, to the gatekeeping screening that *Daubert* demanded.[26] At the very outset of the opinion, Justice Stephen Breyer states:

> We . . . conclude that a trial court may consider one or more of the more specific factors that *Daubert* mentioned when doing so will help determine that testimony's reliability. But, as the Court stated in *Daubert*, the test of reliability is "flexible," and *Daubert*'s list of specific factors neither necessarily nor exclusively applies to all experts or in every case. Rather, the law grants a district court the same broad latitude when it decides how to determine reliability as it enjoys in respect to its ultimate reliability determination.[27]

In *Kumho Tire*, an engineer had offered an opinion on how and why a tire had failed, and in the lawsuit, this expert opinion was relevant to whether the failure was the fault of the manufacturer. Justice Breyer restates his opening theme in the following passage, in which he speaks to the diversity of expert testimony.

> Engineering testimony rests upon scientific foundations, the reliability of which will be at issue in some cases. In other cases, the relevant reliability concerns may focus upon personal knowledge or experience. As the Solicitor General points out, there are many different kinds of experts, and many different kinds of expertise . . . . We agree with the Solicitor General that "[t]he factors identified in *Daubert* may or may not be pertinent in assessing reliability, depending on the nature of the issue, the expert's particular expertise, and the subject of his testimony." The conclusion, in our view, is that we can neither rule out, nor rule in, for all cases and for all time the applicability of the factors mentioned in *Daubert*, nor can we now do so for subsets of cases categorized by category of expert or by kind of evidence. Too much depends upon the particular circumstances of the particular case at issue.[28]

One could read *Kumho Tire* rather narrowly, saying that its language only has relevance to people like engineers, and that for "real science," the four factors remain the key. But this seems erroneous. Whenever science comes into the courtroom, it comes in not as pure theory, but as applied science, and thus looks much like engineering. In court, one asks questions such as "Why did this bridge fall down?" or "Is the blood found at the scene of the crime the defendant's blood?" and so forth. In all such cases, one travels a long path, from pure theory down to a technician in the lab, and the expert in court may combine theory, lab results, personal observations, informed judgment, and more so as to offer relevant and reliable opinions that can aid the trier of fact. Justice Breyer was correct in believing that assessing the use of science in the courtroom is both more complex and more subtle than a focus on the four factors might suggest.

Furthermore, we think that it is good to point out that in all of these cases, evidence was never excluded because the testimony fell on the wrong side of the science versus nonscience line. In none of these cases has the Supreme Court ever said that it intended to police the line between science and nonscience, although a quick reading of the *Daubert* criteria could lead one to believe that they are tempted to set themselves up as authoritative philosophers of science. Instead, the trilogy as a whole makes clear that they intend to police (or more precisely, they intend for trial judges to police) the *application* of science in the courtroom. The effect of the trilogy is to give to the corps of trial judges a task that is difficult, but possible. Since lawyers are not insane, they will generally not present in court witnesses who have no credentials and who have no scientific basis for their testimony. Consequently, trial judges can start with the assumption that good science lurks in the background of the average expert's testimony, and the question will then be how persuasively the witness travels the route from the science to the conclusion.

We hope that our review of the law established by the *Daubert* Trilogy will make it clear why we think that those who have thought about the history, philosophy, and sociology of science should find our topic pertinent to their own concerns. Had the Supreme Court undertaken the task of distinguishing science from nonscience, one could confidently predict that the judicial debates would have become bogged down in sterile and abstract distinctions. Instead, the judiciary seems now to be committed to a different, and far more interesting, task. The question that judges should ask, according to the trilogy, is "How is the science used?" Indeed, to state the question in this way is probably too narrow. As the last case, *Kumho Tire*, made clear, the question lies in how all forms of expertise should be used. And we hope to show in this book that this broader question of the use of expertise is among the most fascinating issues for our time.

OUR METHODOLOGY IN THE NEXT TWO CHAPTERS

In chapters 2 and 3 of this book, we focus on recent opinions by U.S. courts of appeals, which are the intermediate courts between the U.S. Supreme Court, which propounds the general principles, and the U.S. district courts, which try cases. These intermediate tribunals have the major responsibility of trying to implement the principles established by the U.S. Supreme Court. We limit our inquiry to a subset of cases in which the *Daubert* Trilogy was followed, namely, those opinions reversing or rejecting a trial judge's decision on admissibility of an expert (in some cases the trial judge allowed scientific testimony that the appellate panel found inadmissible, and in others the trial judge disallowed testimony found on appeal to be admissible).[29] These types of cases, we believe, usually generate more careful and detailed opinions than do affirmances.[30] In our brief analysis of each case, we identify the problem with the trial judge's understanding of scientific expertise, as explained by the appellate panel. Specifically, we ask whether it was a lack of understanding of the *Daubert* methodological guidelines that caused the problem, or whether there was a failure to understand the social aspects of science. The mixed results of our analyses suggest that an understanding of science includes both an understanding of the methodological aspects of science, and an understanding of the social aspects of science.

NOTES

1. Rebecca Goldstein, *Properties of Light: A Novel* 38 (2001).

2. *See id.* at 39, 69.

3. The term *science wars* refers to "the ever angrier debates about the scope and authority of science." *See* "You Can't Follow the Science Wars without a Battle Map," *Economist*, December 13, 1997, at 77 (the "battle" is between the defenders of science as a linear and progressive affair involving testable and falsifiable descriptions of reality, and critics of science who emphasize its historical, social, rhetorical, political, and even moral and gendered aspects).

4. The *Daubert* Trilogy consists of *Daubert v. Merrell Dow Pharmaceuticals*, 509 U.S. 579 (1993); *General Electric Co. v. Joiner*, 522 U.S. 136 (1997); and *Kumho Tire Co., Ltd. v. Carmichael*, 526 U.S. 137 (1999).

5. *See* David L. Faigman et al., 1 *Modern Scientific Evidence: The Law and Science of Expert Testimony* ix (1997).

6. *See* Michael J. Saks, "The Aftermath of *Daubert*: An Evolving Jurisprudence of Expert Evidence," 40 *Jurimetrics J.* 229, 232–33 (2000).

7. *See* Margaret Farrell, "*Daubert v. Merrell Dow Pharmaceuticals, Inc.*: Epistemiology and Legal Process," 15 *Cardozo L. Rev.* 2183, 2217 (1994).

8. *See* Gary Edmond, "Judicial Representations of Scientific Evidence," 63 *Mod. L. Rev.* 216, (2000).

9. *See generally* David S. Caudill, "Ethnography and the Idealized Accounts of Science in Law," 39 *San Diego L. Rev.* 269 (2002).

10. *See, e.g.*, Ronald J. Allen and Brian Leiter, "Naturalized Epistemology and the Law of Evidence," 87 *Va. L. Rev.* 1491, 1492 (2001) (dismissing "the unfortunate fascination in some quarters of the legal academy with 'postmodern' conceptions of

knowledge and truth, conceptions notable for their superficiality and for the fact that almost no philosophers subscribe to them"), 1492 n1 (postmodern skepticism "about the possibility of objective truth, as well as our capacity to find objective truth in the world," is "remarkably useless for evidence law").

11. Johannes Fabian, *Time and the Other: How Anthropology Makes Its Object* 109 (1983).

12. *See* Anthony Giddens, *Modernity and Self-Identity: Self and Society in the Late Modern Age* 7 (1991), quoted in Alan Irwin and Brian Wynne, "Conclusions," in *Misunderstanding Science? The Public Reconstruction of Science and Technology* (eds. Alan Irwin and Brian Wynne, 1996), at 219 (scientific "claims to authority are likely to be met with an increasingly critical (if not downright hostile) audience" in public contexts).

13. 509 U.S. 579 (1993).

14. *Daubert*, 509 U.S. at 593.

15. *See id.* ("we do not presume to set out a definitive checklist or test").

16. *See* 509 U.S. at 594.

17. *See* 509 U.S. at 592–93 (trial judge must make a "preliminary assessment of whether . . . [the] reasoning and methodology properly can be applied to the facts in issue").

18. If one puts emphasis on Justice Blackmun's use of the word "can," then one can say that the trial judge is to ask only whether the methodology can be properly applied, not whether it actually has been. But this distinction is cutting it fine, and the Supreme Court's subsequent cases did not try to draw such a fine line.

19. 522 U.S. 136 (1997).

20. *See* 522 U.S. at 141–42, 146.

21. *See* 522 U.S. at 144–46.

22. *See* 522 U.S. at 143 ("the Court of Appeals erred [in] applying an overly stringent review . . . [and] failed to give the trial court the deference that is the hallmark of abuse-of-discretion review").

23. *See id.*

24. 526 U.S. 137 (1999).

25. *See* 526 U.S. at 147 (Rule 702 "makes no relevant distinction between scientific knowledge and technical or other specialized knowledge").

26. *See* 526 U.S. at 148 (*Daubert* "gatekeeping" is not limited to "scientific" knowledge).

27. 526 U.S. at 141–42.

28. 526 U.S. at 150.

29. Our research methodology was simply to read all the recent federal cases (applying *Daubert*) in which a circuit court reversed a district court judge's decision with respect to admissibility of an expert. We wanted to identify and focus on cases concerning reliability, therefore we did not consider the numerous cases concerning relevance (i.e., determinations that the evidence would not assist the trier of fact), the distinction between lay and expert testimony, or the danger of prejudice outweighing probative value or of jury confusion. We also did not consider cases in which (i) the trial judge failed to hold a *Daubert* hearing, and (ii) the trial judge made no findings

that indicated why an expert's testimony was admitted or disallowed. Finally, we eliminated some cases concerning reliability if that issue was so mixed with other issues (e.g., relevance) that the finding of reliability (or unreliability) was not determinative. In short, the recent cases analyzed in this book are those in which a primary disagreement (between the trial judge and the appellate panel) over the reliability of an expert was identifiable *and* discussed in the appellate opinion.

30. We are sympathetic to the charge that "an empirical analysis of published case law is, by its very nature, restricted to an analysis of post hoc justifications . . . and does not fully capture the judicial decision-making process," *see* Gatowski et al., "Asking the Gatekeepers: A National Survey of Judges on Judging Expert Evidence in a Post-*Daubert* World," 25 *Law and Hum. Behav.* 433, 434 (2001), but we believe that more of the "judicial decision-making process" is revealed in reversals.

Chapter Two

On Judges Who Are Too Strict

SKEPTICISM FROM IDEALIZATION

Recent cases demonstrate that some trial judges are overly skeptical of scientific experts, and strangely enough, this skepticism can spring from idealizing science. This error of excessive skepticism has a general form:

> Premise: All scientists follow a perfect methodology.
> Premise: This witness did not follow a perfect methodology.
> Conclusion: This witness is not a scientist.

The first premise is obviously false. Scientists do the best they can, and perfection is unattainable. The alternative view is that science is a pragmatic activity, and experts ought to be judged according to the local practices in their field. For example, an expert's testimony should not be rejected solely because it is based on less-than-perfect information, or involves alternative explanations, or is inconclusive except in probabilistic terms.

The error of expecting perfection is often joined by a second error:

> Fact: Two experts disagree.
> Premise: There is only one truth.
> Premise: A competent scientist will report the truth.
> Conclusion: One of the witnesses is . . . lying, corrupt, a junk scientist, and so forth.

The second premise is obviously false, at least insofar as we have no unequivocal access to undisputed truth. Moreover, most scientific inquiry generates probability, not certainty—competent scientists report probabilities. The alternative to the idealization error is the view that good scientists often disagree, and that controversial evidence—for example, fingerprint evidence—is sometimes useful even if it is only probabilistic.

The federal courts of appeals (typically, a three-judge panel hears appeals) have seemingly tried to avoid these errors, and below we identify in their recent opinions a modest or pragmatic perspective on the scientific enterprise. Our use of the term *pragmatism*, however, merits a preliminary explanation.

WHAT IS PRAGMATISM?

We recognize that defining the term *pragmatism* is hopeless, and so we use this word in its informal and colloquial sense. Indeed, defining pragmatism as an orientation or approach is as difficult as defining formalism or realism. Anthony D'Amato attempts to introduce *legal* pragmatism, in his *Analytic Jurisprudence Anthology* (1996), by offering helpful excerpts from the writings of John Dewey, Oliver Wendell Holmes, Richard Rorty, and Judge Richard Posner, and from his own work.[1] Posner is particularly familiar and succinct:

> Pragmatism in the sense that I find congenial means looking at problems concretely, experimentally, without illusions, with a full awareness of the limitations of human reason, with a sense of the "localness" of human knowledge, the difficulty of translations between cultures, the unattainability of "truth," the consequent importance of keeping diverse paths of inquiry open, the dependence of inquiry on culture and social institutions, and above all the insistence that social thought and action be evaluated as instruments to valued human goals rather than as ends in themselves.[2]

Posner also associates pragmatism with the "scientific spirit . . . of inquiry, challenge, fallibilism, open-mindedness, respect for fact, and acceptance of change."[3] Such "respect for fact" alongside "open-mindedness" hints at a pragmatic perspective on science as neither realist (facts = nature) nor relativist (facts as merely social constructs), but as oriented to local, practical problem solving.

Moreover, the implied rejection by pragmatists of over-arching theoretical frameworks destabilizes any attempt to define pragmatism as a theoretical framework. In D'Amato's formulation: "It is hard to define Pragmatism, as it well might be, because Pragmatists dislike definitions. Definitions are themselves formal, suggesting logic and exactitude . . . . A definition, to a Pragmatist, is just a rule of thumb."[4] D'Amato's introduction to pragmatism is thus itself pragmatic: a matter of tendencies that can only be captured in specific solutions to particular problems.

Finally, because we want to distinguish a pragmatic perspective on science from philosophical or legal pragmatism generally, we need to construct that pragmatic perspective even though there is no unified view among philosophers of science as to what pragmatism in science entails. Thomas Nickles, for example, reads Kuhn's paradigm theory

> as retreating from a realist, "Truth Now" account to a sort of pragmatism in which the *solved problem* rather than the true theory becomes the unit of achievement in science . . . . [Kuhn's] stress on the local contexts of research and the constraints they impose on thought and action are very important.[5]

Michael Ruse identifies his own tendency to be "somewhat of a pragmatist, a nonrealist of a kind," since he thinks "advance means getting one's theory more in tune with values like consilience [*sic*] than progress towards knowledge of a metaphysical reality."[6] Finally, Karin Knorr-Cetina, a sociologist of science, considers the focus on scientific practices, in contrast to producing normative philosophy of science or rational accounts of theory choice, to be pragmatic—"you don't always try to find the mechanisms *behind* things without considering what is on the surface."[7] These aphorisms, by emphasizing local practices and contexts instead of global reality or truth, are useful in our own assessment of a pragmatic trend in law and science relations.

We should also distinguish our use of the term from that of philosopher David Resnik, who has proposed a pragmatic approach to the demarcation problem (i.e., how to distinguish science from nonscience), and even offered it as a framework for judicial analyses of scientific validity. Resnik states that the demarcation problem (which we think is a nonproblem in law) remains a point of controversy not only among historians, philosophers, and sociologists of science, but in practical settings such as in the use of scientific testing in the courtroom.[8] Historically, positivistic verifiability criteria gave way to Popper's falsification thesis—scientific theories are testable—but critics argued that the thesis provides neither necessary nor sufficient conditions for classifying statements as scientific.[9] Resnik therefore surveys historical, sociological, political, psychological, and epistemological approaches, none of which develop "necessary and sufficient conditions for distinguishing between science and non-science." Science, he concludes, cannot be defined in this way, because we "distinguish between science and non-science in the context of making practical decisions and choices."[10]

> [T]o distinguish between science and non-science, we must know who is seeking to make the distinction and why . . . . We can reject some definitions because they do not do a good job of promoting our goals and interests . . . .[11]

In the legal system, a conservative and rigid definition of science, emphasizing reliability and rational consensus, seems to set useful limits on the costs and durations of trials, and to prevent mistakes, like wrongful convictions; but that definition "might prevent an innocent person from gaining access to theories, concepts, and data that could exonerate that person." For Resnik, therefore, we should "evaluate definitions of science in light of their probable effects on justice, due process, efficiency, and other goals of the legal system." If that sounds relativistic, Resnik does not claim that the definition of science rests only on practical concerns.

> There are some common themes that should run through these different definitions of science, [including] testability, empirical support, progressiveness, problem-solving ability, and so on . . . . [One] can hold that there are some general criteria for distinguishing between science and non-science while holding that particular judgments . . . depend on contextual features, such as practical goals and concerns.[12]

Resnik's proposed pragmatism is similar to, but does not quite capture, the pragmatic view of science that we identify in recent federal cases applying *Daubert.*

COURTS ADOPT SCIENTIFIC, NOT LEGAL, PRAGMATISM

David Resnik seems to be recommending pragmatism on the part of judges by saying that when they *choose* their definition of science, they should "evaluate definitions of science in light of their probable effects on justice, due process, efficiency, and other goals of the legal system." Thus, in Resnik's account, judges might *choose* a rigid, conservative view of science, or a more liberal one that emphasizes "problem-solving ability, testability, or other, less rigid criteria."[13] Resnik's argument is reminiscent of social constructivist arguments in the wake of *Daubert*—consider Margaret Farrell's argument that law should construct its own truths rather than follow scientific constructs, because facts in each field serve different purposes.[14] That style of pragmatism, whatever its merits, does not seem to be in fashion among federal judges. Rather, judges seem to be adopting a pragmatist view of the scientific enterprise itself: naturalistic but representational, useful but model-based, rigorous but approximate, social but empirical, evidence-based but probabilistic. That framework, and its contrast with both (i) an idealized (i.e., realist, verificationist, or rationalist) view of science, and (ii) Resnik's pragmatically constructed "legal" science, will become clearer in our analysis of some recent cases. One who holds a pragmatic view of science

A. realizes that expertise does not always rely on objective measurement, but often on other investigative techniques (e.g., patient narratives, interviews)

B. recognizes that science often involves uncertainty, teamwork, and alternative explanatory models
C. acknowledges that science is probabilistic, not certain
D. understands that not all scientific knowledge appears in peer-reviewed journals
E. does not reject social science solely on the basis of its methodological limitations

We will now discuss five cases to illustrate points A through E. We realize that this sort of catalog can become tedious, but we take this risk so as to avoid being overly abstract. We hope that the details of these cases will make the abstract thesis come alive.

Medical Diagnosis Often Relies on Patient Reports, Not on Objective Measurement Techniques

In *Cooper v. Carl E. Nelson and Co.*,[15] a case brought by an injured worker seeking damages for an accident at a construction site, the plaintiff's medical experts relied on the plaintiff's statements about his past medical history as the basis for their diagnosis. The trial court decided the testimony was not admissible "because the physicians had an inadequate foundation"—no scientific basis—for "evaluating the cause of Mr. Cooper's injury." The court of appeals reversed, finding the district court "assumed an overly aggressive role as 'gatekeeper'":

> [I]n clinical medicine, the methodology of physical examination and self-reported medical history employed by Dr. Richardson is generally appropriate. . . . [The defendant] suggests no alternative that could be employed by the conscientious clinical physician in this situation.[16]

Whether the doctor failed to consider other factors in the plaintiff's life related to "the onset of the condition," and whether the medical history was accurate, were both "quite susceptible to exploration and cross-examination"; they went to the weight, not the admissibility, of the testimony. The methodology of a physician employing "the accepted diagnostic tool of examination accompanied by the physical history as related by the patient" was acceptable under *Daubert*. The appellate panel in *Cooper* therefore emphasized the actual practices of clinical physicians rather than setting up, as the trial judge did, an idealized scientific basis as a standard to be met. Sometimes the data relied upon by experts comes from interviews, and as long as that is a "standard investigating technique" in the field—as in arson cases—we should not demand more.[17]

Science Involves Uncertainty, Teamwork, and Alternative Explanatory Models

In *Walker v. Soo Line Railroad Company*,[18] an appellate panel likewise focused on the actual practices of experts to reverse a trial judge's exclusion of testimony as lacking a scientific basis. The plaintiff, Walker, claiming injury on a tower during an electrical storm, tried to introduce the testimony of three experts: Dr. Pliskin (a psychologist), Dr. Capelli-Schelpfeffer (an expert on electrical trauma), and Dr. Uman (an expert on electrical safety). Dr. Pliskin's evaluation of the decline in Walker's IQ was excluded at trial because Pliskin "relied on medical, educational, and professional histories reported by" Walker and his "girlfriend," some of which the trial judge found to be inaccurate. The appellate panel, however, noting that medical "professionals reasonably may be expected to rely on self-reported patient histories," found Pliskin's scientific methodology to be acceptable under *Daubert* (and again, any inaccuracies could be explored in cross-examination). Moreover, the defendant's argument on appeal that Dr. Pliskin's testimony was inadmissible because he did "not state definitively that the electrical trauma caused the drop in Mr. Walker's IQ" was rejected, suggesting that admissible testimony (which might be useful to the jury) does not imply certainty as to ultimate issues.[19]

Dr. Capelli-Schelpfeffer's testimony was also excluded at trial, seemingly because she relied "on the work of her team members in forming her opinion" that Walker suffered from post-traumatic stress disorder.[20] The appellate panel again found that practice to be common:

> Medical professionals have long been expected to rely on the opinions of other medical professionals in forming their opinions . . . . Indeed, courts frequently have pointed to an expert's reliance on the reports of others as an indication that their testimony is reliable.[21]

The appellate panel also rejected the defendant's argument that Capelli-Schelpfeffer's testimony was unreliable because she relied on Pliskin's work but disagreed with his conclusion:

> That two different experts reach opposing conclusions from the same information does not render their opinions inadmissible . . . . "Merely because two qualified experts reach directly opposite conclusions using similar, if not identical, data bases . . . does not necessarily mean that, under *Daubert*, one opinion is *per se* unreliable."[22]

Finally, the appellate panel confirmed that although Capelli-Schelpfeffer was not a psychiatrist, her testimony about post-traumatic stress disorder was admissible because she was the leader of a clinical medical team:

> The team approach to medical diagnosis and treatment is employed to ensure that all relevant disciplines work together for the good of the patient. The leader . . . reconcile[s], when necessary, competing perspectives. In short, the expertise of the team leader is to evaluate, in light of the overall picture, the contributions of each member of the team.[23]

That picture of experts from various disciplines with "competing perspectives," each of whom offers a limited contribution, betrays a view of science as not only methodological, but also social, institutional, and rhetorical.

The trial judge in *Walker* also barred the testimony of Dr. Uman—about the different ways that lightning could have penetrated the tower in which the plaintiff was stationed—as too speculative. The appellate panel, however, found his testimony scientifically valid since experts "are allowed to posit alternate models to explain their conclusion."[24] All of these conclusions by the court of appeals regarding the plaintiff's experts in *Walker* suggest that the trial judge mischaracterized the scientific enterprise as a field of objective measurement, definitive (or uncontradictable) conclusions, individual achievement, and singular explanatory models; for the appellate panel, however, the practices of experts were seen to often involve data from subjective narratives, an inability to conclude (and even contradictory conclusions), teamwork, and alternative explanatory models. Like the pragmatists that they are, scientists work with what they have, and with others, to produce the best and most useful knowledge.

Science Is Probabilistic, Not Certain

In *Jahn v. Equine Services, PSC*,[25] a veterinary malpractice case, the plaintiff's experts could not "identify with any degree of certainty the specific physiological cause" of a race horse's death, and one expert lacked relevant surgical experience. The trial judge therefore ruled their testimony inadmissible under *Daubert*, but the appellate panel held that "the district court's *Daubert* analysis both mischaracterized the methodology employed" by the experts "and ultimately employed a standard of admissibility more stringent than that expressed in Rule 702."

> In order to be admissible on the issue of causation, an expert's testimony need not eliminate all other possible causes of the injury . . . . *Daubert* and [Federal Rule of Evidence] 702 require only that the expert testimony be derived from inferences based on a scientific method and that those inferences be derived from the facts of the case at hand . . . .[26]

Because the defendants' medical records were not complete, *certainty* was "not to be found in this case." While the trial court viewed the experts' testimony as "stacking one guess on top of another," both experts (by necessity) "based their opinions on the facts with which they were presented." If the trial judge had explored whether the testimony reflected "the same level of intellectual rigor that characterizes" veterinary practice, it would have been clear that the experts "used a methodology derived from scientific medical knowledge, although limited by the information provided to them . . . ."[27] Moreover, the trial judge's suspicion of testimony that contradicted a pathologist's report was inappropriate: "determining which is more credible should be left for the trier of fact and . . . not considered when ruling on Rule 702 admissibility." Finally, looking "at test results and physical symptoms to infer the presence of an infection" is *not* a methodologically unsound "assumption" or "guess"—it is a diagnosis. Here again, compared to the trial court's image of scientific knowledge, the view of the appellate court seems deflationary— sometimes science is "less than certain," sometimes scientists necessarily piece together a probable series of events under less-than-ideal circumstances, and sometimes their admissible conclusions are shaky, challengeable, or less persuasive than at other times.[28]

Not All Scientific Knowledge Is Peer Reviewed and Published

In *Smith v. Ford Motor Company*,[29] the plaintiff proposed to call two experts to support his claim that the steering mechanism in his van malfunctioned, causing an accident. The trial court concluded (i) that the experts were not qualified to testify because they were not automotive engineers, and (ii) that their methodologies were unreliable because they had not been peer reviewed. On the first point, the appellate panel held that the experts' expertise did not concern the ultimate issue, which could require an automotive engineer, but that their expertise could nevertheless be "relevant to evaluating" other factual matters. On the second point, peer review, the appellate panel held that

> the district court did not indicate whether publication is typical for the type of methodology these experts purported to employ. The district court merely recited the failure of the experts to publish and concluded that their testimony was unreliable.[30]

The keys, for the appellate panel, were (i) whether "well-established engineering practices" were applied, and (ii) whether the methodology was based on "extensive practical experience," *not* whether "a single, potentially irrelevant criterion" was met. Ideally, publication in peer-reviewed journals is relevant, but actual practices "in the relevant engineering and accident analysis communities" are sometimes more relevant.[31] Again, the trial judge's idealization of formal scientific practices eclipsed any inquiry into how experts actually work.

The Limitations of Social Science Do Not Make It Unscientific

Finally, in *United States v. Smithers*, the trial court excluded the testimony of Dr. Solomon Fulero, an expert on eyewitness identification, on the basis that his opinion was not scientifically valid. A divided appellate panel reversed, confirming that psychological studies of the limitations of perception and memory in eyewitness identification are now a "scientifically sound and proper subject of expert testimony."[32] The strong and lengthy dissenting opinion in support of the trial judge's skepticism is interesting because of its criticism not only of research on the deficiencies of eyewitness identification but of social science generally.

> The trepidation with which nearly all appellate courts have treated [expert testimony on eyewitness identifications] is representative of a broader reluctance . . . to admit the expert testimony of social scientists with the same deference given to the testimony of those in the physical sciences . . . . [D]isagreements between dueling experts in the physical sciences . . . typically focus on the data . . . which is subject to objective analysis. The certainty of the testimony of social scientists, however, is limited by the nature of their field.[33]

A majority of the panel, nevertheless, was less reluctant, which suggests less idealism concerning the hard sciences together with a pragmatic acceptance of the limitations of the social sciences. Science is thus not characterized by its objectivity or certainty—and conclusions are seen as often tentative, contradictory, or probabilistic. This does not signal unreliability, but rather marks the typical conditions under which natural *and* social scientists work to produce useful knowledge.

IDEALIZING METHODOLOGY

The foregoing five cases all involved trial judges whose decisions not to admit certain expert testimony were reversed, and we have introduced our argument that the misunderstandings on the part of the trial judges were not primarily methodological, but rather reflected misunderstandings as to social aspects of the practice of science. Of course, we concede that there are some recent cases that exemplify the need for trial judges to better understand scientific methodology. For example, the trial judge in *Hardyman v. Norfolk and Western Railway Company*,[34] a Federal Employers Liability Act suit based on a carpal tunnel syndrome (CTS) injury, excluded the testimony of the plaintiff's experts on causation. One such expert, Dr. Douglas Linz, employed differential diagnosis methodology—considering all potential causes of symptoms and then (by tests and examinations) eliminating likely causes until the most probable one is isolated—to reach his conclusion that plaintiff's CTS was caused by work activities. The trial judge, after acknowledging the acceptability of differential diagnoses, "failed to recognize that Dr. Linz applied [that] method . . . [and the judge] seemed actually to reject this method . . . ." The appellate panel therefore reversed, "convinced that the rationale of the district court did not justify exclusion of Plaintiff's expert testimony."[35]

On the other hand, in contrast to the trial judge in *Hardyman* who did not recognize or accept sound methodology, the trial judges in the five cases we discussed above exemplify a different problem, which might be called the idealization of scientific methodology. That is, the *reason* why those judges did not recognize the practical goals and limitations of science—in other words, its (i) reliance on self-reported medical history, (ii) uncertainty, (iii) competing explanations, and (iv) conventional practices—was their idealized image of the features of the scientific enterprise: objective measurement, definitive conclusions, and unanimous consensus in peer-reviewed publications. Our assertion that trial judges should have a somewhat deflated image of science might, we understand, sound counterintuitive. It would seem that to appropriate the best science in law, judges should set a very high standard. Because we want to challenge that notion, we turn now to six recent cases that specifically highlight the problem of idealizing science, namely, that by doing so the best science may be kept out of the courtroom. Again, in each of these cases, trial judges were reversed by appellate panels who understood the social, institutional, and rhetorical context of expertise. In their pragmatic view of science,

A. Science is a social practice reflecting the relevant scientific community's goals and standards.
B. Science evolves on the basis of reasonable beliefs and resolution of internal debates.
C. Methodological standards are often mediated by pragmatic limitations.
D. Science is a historical, interested, and economic phenomenon.

Science Reflects the Goals and Standards of Particular Communities of Scientists

In *Alfred v. Caterpillar, Inc.*,[36] a products liability action against the manufacturer of a paver, the plaintiff's safety expert was excluded because the trial judge found "his opinion is simply not competent under *Daubert* [i.e.,] it is not supported by sufficient testing, experience, background, education, or thought. . . ." The appellate panel, however, was "persuaded that [the expert's] testimony . . . was reliable . . . because it was the result of having researched and applied [well-accepted] standards [in the engineering community]." The trial judge's comments that the expert's opinion was "very limited" and "backed by very little work and very limited expertise" suggest that the judge wanted more of science that this expert could offer; the appellate panel's reaction was to look at what the community of such experts think and do.[37] Expertise, that is, reflects social practice, not just an abstract, methodological ideal. Indeed, even methodological ideals are local and dependent on the relevant community's standards. Thus, in Charles Alan Taylor's formulation, an empirical conclusion by a scientist

> is itself pragmatically contingent on wider configurations of practices. . . .
>
> My point is not that all interpretations of the facts are of equal legitimacy [, but we should reject] the claim that the relative legitimacy of a given interpretation is a natural condition of the material to be interpreted, rather than a function of the audience's [e.g., a scientific community's] evaluations of the evidence adduced on its behalf. . . .[38]

Recourse to the social and institutional aspects of science, in contrast to abstract ideals, is also evident in five more cases where a trial judge's idealization of science was corrected.

Science Is Based on Reasonable Belief and Is Subject to Internal Disagreements

In *United States v. Finley*,[39] the trial judge in a criminal trial excluded the defendant's psychological expert's testimony on the basis that "the testimony would not be helpful to the jury."[40] According to the appellate panel, the trial judge "seemed troubled by the fact that the psychological tests did not reveal a conclusive diagnosis," and by the fact that the expert "based his opinion on his belief that [the defendant] was not faking or being deceptive." The expert even admitted at the *Daubert* hearing that his diagnosis was "extremely gray." Reversing the conviction, the appellate panel implied that the trial judge was asking for too much:

> It appears from the record before us that [the expert] based his diagnosis on proper psychological methodology and reasoning. . . . [He] did not base his conclusions solely on [the defendant's] statements; rather, he used his many years of experience. . . . Based on his clinical experience, [the expert] concluded that

[the defendant] was not faking or lying. A belief, supported by sound reasoning, . . . is sufficient to support the reliability of a mental health diagnosis. . . . We have recognized that the concepts of mental disorders are "constantly-evolving conception[s]" about which "the psychological and psychiatric community is far from unanimous.". . .[41]

Here again is a picture of science as inconclusive, based on reasonable belief, evolving, and subject to internal disagreements; this is not, however, a critical assessment of scientific reliability, but an acknowledgment that science is a social enterprise with institutional supports (e.g., standardized diagnostic categories) and debates that betray rhetorical strategies on the part of scientists.

Methodological Standards Are Often Mediated by Pragmatic Concerns and Limitations

Trial judges who want more from science, we might say, need to understand more about its limitations, and their exclusive focus on idealized methodological aspects—like testing or data—might be misleading them. For example, in *Pipitone v. Biomatrix, Inc.*,[42] a patient who contracted a salmonella infection after receiving a knee injection brought a products liability action against the manufacturer of the synthetic fluid Synvisc. At trial, the testimony of an infectious disease expert was disallowed as unreliable because (i) no epidemiological study was performed, (ii) no published study supported his opinion, and (iii) other potential sources for an infection had not been eliminated. As to the first statement, the appellate panel agreed with the expert that an epidemiological study "is not necessary or appropriate in a case such as this in which only one person is infected." As to the lack of peer-reviewed literature supporting the expert's opinion, the appellate panel observed that where

> there is no evidence that anyone has ever contracted a salmonella infection from an injection of any kind into the knee, it is difficult to see why a scientist would study this phenomenon. We conclude . . . that the lack of reports . . . *supports* [the] conclusion that the infection did not arise due to [a] source not related to Synvisc.[43]

Even the third concern, that other sources were not eliminated, was rejected by the appellate panel:

> [The expert] methodically eliminated the alternative sources of the infection as viable possibilities. After doing so, he stated that he was "99.9 percent" sure that the source of the salmonella was the Synvisc syringe.[44]

Significantly, the expert seemed to fare badly under the four *Daubert* guidelines: (i) he "did not test his hypothesis," (ii) no "known or potential rate of error or controlling standard [was] associated with [his] hypothesis," (iii) there was no "relevant scientific literature," and (iv) only his diagnostic principles, not his particular hypothesis, were "generally accepted in the relevant scientific community." Nevertheless, the appellate panel deemed it

> appropriate for the trial court to consider factors other than those listed in *Daubert* to evaluate . . . reliability . . . . In this case, the expert's testimony is based mainly on his personal observations, professional experience, education and training.[45]

A similar evaluation by an appellate panel appeared in *Furry v. Bielomatik, Inc.*,[46] where a safety engineer's testimony was excluded because he did not offer specific designs for safety features that he identified as necessary. The appellate panel vacated a summary judgment because the trial court's evaluation "appears to have been based on an overly expansive view of [the expert's] role as a safety expert, as well as an overly technical application of the factors articulated in . . . *Daubert*."[47] In *Pipitone* and *Furry*, the *Daubert* guidelines emerge as ideals that must be mediated by pragmatic concerns because every hypothesis will not have been supported by or the subject of extensive testing, well-established standards or error rates, peer-reviewed publication, or even consensus (except in the most general sense of consensus regarding methodological principles).

Science Is a Historical, Interested, and Economic Phenomenon

Two other recent cases also highlight the limitations under which science pragmatically, though not ideally, operates. In *Lauzon v. Senco Products Inc.*,[48] the trial court excluded the testimony of a forensic engineer who testified often in pneumatic nail gun cases. The trial judge found (i) the testing of the expert's theory inadequate (the expert was unable to duplicate the events of the accident on which the case was based), (ii) the relevant peer-reviewed literature inadequate, (iii) the expert's theory not widely accepted, and, impliedly, (iv) the expert's research not sufficiently independent of litigation. The appellate panel found the expert's testing and the literature (and therefore general acceptance) sufficient, but also observed that the expert's involvement with past litigation did not infect his research.[49]

> [T]he slight negative impact of [forensic engineer] Kelsey's introduction to the field of pneumatic nail guns through litigation is outweighed by his independent research, independent testimony, and adherence to the underlying rationale of the general acceptance factor, scientific reliability.[50]

General acceptance cannot be found for every reliable hypothesis, nor can many reliable hypotheses be found outside the litigation context. Moreover, as explained in *Metabolife International, Inc. v. Wornick*,[51] a study that is commissioned by a party, is not subjected to peer review, and is incomplete is not by those facts alone rendered unreliable:

> Rather than disqualify the study because of "incompleteness" [the overall project was ongoing, but all of the relevant data had been gathered in final form] or because it was commissioned by Metabolife, the district court [on remand] should examine the soundness of the methodology employed.[52]

These cases suggest that science is not pure—there is always funding from somewhere, and there is always a social or contextual reason to study something. In *Pipitone*, there was no reason to study salmonella knee infections until the injury occurred; in *Furry*, there was no history of extensive testing, and therefore no well-established error rate or consensus concerning the safety of "paper converting" machines; and in *Lauzon* and *Metabolife*, the relevant research was driven by litigation. These factors do not signal unreliability, but rather constitute social features of science. In effect, the trial judge in each of these cases understood the methodological ideals of science, but not its historical, communal, and economic dimensions. To the extent that the trial judges at least recognized these social features of science, the features were viewed as problems or impurities rather than as conventions or inevitabilities—that is what we mean by the tendency to idealize science. While no one doubts that the scientific enterprise rests on social structures, some trial judges tend to see methodology as a check on the effects of those structures. The notion that methodology itself is social is therefore counterintuitive.

The problem of judicial idealization of science, in the cases just discussed, resulted in reversals because the experts, engaged in a pragmatic enterprise with practical goals and limitations, did not live up to the trial judge's ideals. In the next chapter, we discuss a parallel problem: trial judges are often reversed for deferring to the social authority of experts, even when the experts lack methodological reliability. As we will show, the debate about whether judges should defer to science out of ignorance or, on the other hand, should demand that experts educate the judge, is not new. We argue that when trial judges understand the *social*, and not just the *methodological*, authority of science, as well as the potential disconnect between social authority and reliability, they tend to adopt an educational model of their gatekeeping responsibilities.

NOTES

1. See *Analytic Jurisprudence Anthology* 219–48 (ed. Anthony D'Amato, 1996). See *also* "Symposium on the Renaissance of Pragmatism in American/Legal

Thought," 63 *S. Cal. L. Rev.* 1569–1853 (1990), which includes articles by Thomas C. Grey, Martha Minow and Elizabeth V. Spelman, Judge Richard A. Posner, Hilary Putnam, Margaret Jane Radin, Catherine Wells, and Cornel West, as well as commentary by Scott Brewer, Mari J. Matsuda, Frank Michelman, Ruth Anna Putnam, Richard Rorty, Joseph William Singer, and Marion Smiley.

2. *See* Richard Posner, *The Problems of Jurisprudence* 465 (1990), quoted in *Analytic Jurisprudence, supra* note 1, at 239.

3. *See* Posner, *supra* note 2, at 465.

4. *See Analytic Jurisprudence, supra* note 1, at 219 (D'Amato's introduction to chapter 6, the readings on pragmatism). The problem of defining pragmatism is echoed in H. S. Thayer's entry "Pragmatism" in 6 *The Encyclopedia of Philosophy* 431 (1967):

> In addition to some uncertainty as to the facts in the evolution of pragmatism [the familiar origin story is that Charles Peirce, William James, and others founded the Metaphysical Club in the 1870s at Cambridge], there are . . . several problems of interpretation. Peirce and James often gave very different accounts of what they meant by "pragmatism". . . .
>
> [Pragmatism], by virtue of being an evolving philosophical movement, is to be viewed as a group of associated theoretical ideas and attitudes developed over a period of time and exhibiting . . . rather significant shifts in direction and in formulation. . . .
>
> . . . Schiller, in an almost intoxicating pluralistic spirit, commented that there were as many pragmatisms as there were pragmatists. . . .

5. *See* Werner Callebaut, *Taking the Naturalist Turn, or, How Real Philosophy of Science Is Done* 53 (1993) (interview with Nickles).

6. *See id.* at 469 (interview with Ruse).

7. *See id.* at 120–21 (interview with Knorr-Cetina).

8. *See* David B. Resnik, "A Pragmatic Approach to the Demarcation Problem," 31 *Stud. Hist. Phil. Sci.* 249–50 (2000).

9. *See id.* at 253. The Court in *Daubert* cited Popper in support of "testability," the first prong of the four-part test (testability, low error-rate, publication, and general acceptance). *See* 509 U.S. at 593.

10. *See* Resnik, *supra* note 8, at 254–58.

11. *Id.* at 262.

12. *See id.* at 263–64.

13. *See id.* at 263.

14. *See* Farrell, "*Daubert v. Merrell Dow Pharmaceuticals, Inc.*: Epistemiology and Legal Process," 15 *Cardozo L. Rev.* 2183, 2204–5 (1994).

15. 211 F.3d 1008 (7th Cir. 2000).

16. *See* 211 F.3d at 1012, 1019–20.

17. *See* 211 F.3d at 1020–21, citing *United States v. Lundy*, 809 F.2d 392, 395–96 (7th Cir. 1987) (arson experts regularly rely on interviews with witnesses).

18. 208 F.3d 581 (7th Cir. 2000).

19. *See* 208 F.3d at 585–87.

20. *See* 209 F.3d at 588. We say "seemingly" excluded because "the district court's reasons for exclusion" were "not stated with optimal clarity." *See id.*

21. *Id.*, citing *Birdsell v. United States*, 346 F.2d 775, 779–80 (5th Cir. 1965).

22. *Id*. at 588–89, quoting *Allapattah Servs., Inc. v. Exxon Corp.*, 61 F. Supp. 2d 1335, 1341 (S.D. Fla. 1999).

23. *Id*.

24. *See* 208 F.3d at 589.

25. 233 F.3d 382 (6th Cir. 2000).

26. 233 F.3d at 387, 389–90.

27. *See* F.3d at 390–91, quoting *Kumho Tire*, 526 U.S. at 152.

28. *See* 233 F.3d at 391–93.

29. 215 F.3d 713 (7th Cir. 2000).

30. *See* 215 F.3d at 720.

31. *See* 215 F.3d at 720–21.

32. 212 F.3d 306, 310–13 (6th Cir. 2000).

33. *See* 212 F.3d at 327–28 (Batchelder, J., dissenting).

34. 243 F.3d 255 (6th Cir. 2001).

35. *See* 243 F.3d at 257, 261–62, 267.

36. 262 F.3d 1083 (10th Cir. 2001).

37. *See* 262 F.3d at 1086–88.

38. Charles Alan Taylor, "Feuding Communities and the Feudalism of Science: Democratizing the Community and/of Science," in *Rhetoric and Community: Studies in Unity and Fragmentation* (ed. J. Michael Hogan, 1998), at 289.

39. 301 F.3d 1000 (9th Cir. 2002).

40. *Id*. at 1006–7 ("the jury could independently determine [the defendant's] credibility"). A second ground for exclusion, not discussed here, was as a sanction, but the court held that either basis was sufficient to exclude the testimony. *See id*.

41. *Id*. at 1008–12 (quoting *United States v. Rahn*, 993 F.2d 1405, 1411 [9th Cir. 1993]).

42. 288 F.3d 239 (5th Cir. 2002).

43. *See* 288 F.3d at 241, 245–46.

44. *See* 288 F.3d at 248.

45. *See* 288 F.3d at 245–47.

46. 32 Fed. Appx. 882 (9th Cir. 2002) (unpublished opinion).

47. *See id*. at *1.

48. 270 F.3d 681 (8th Cir. 2001).

49. *See* 270 F.3d at 688–92. "An expert's finding that flows from research independent of litigation is less likely to be biased and the expert is limited to 'the degree to which he can tailor his testimony to serve a party's interest.'" 270 F.3d at 692, quoting *Daubert v. Merrell Dow Pharmaceuticals*, 43 F.3d 1311, 1317 (9th Cir. 1995), citing Peter W. Huber, *Galileo's Revenge: Junk Science in the Courtroom* 206–7 (1991).

50. *See* 270 F.3d at 693.

51. 264 F.3d 832 (9th Cir. 2001).

52. See 264 F.3d at 843.

Chapter Three

On Judges Who Are Too Gullible

DEFERENCE FROM IDEALIZATION

Recent cases demonstrate that some trial judges are overly deferential to scientific experts, which deference springs naturally from idealizing science. This error of excessive deference has a general form:

> Premise: Science gives us the truth.
> Premise: This witness is a scientist.
> Conclusion: This witness will give us the truth.

The first premise is obviously false; science gives us probabilities. And the second premise is too simplistic because not all scientists are equal. Some trial judges, nevertheless, make the error of excessive deference because of the social authority of science in contemporary culture. The mere presence of credentials in an established field can tempt judges to accept testimony that is less than reliable. In this chapter, we demonstrate how courts of appeals have tried to correct the error of excessive deference.

ARE JUDGES EQUIPPED TO JUDGE SCIENCE?

> I think that judges can become "comfortable" with science or scientists if they know more about how they operate . . . . [T]here has been this notion that science is beyond us, in another world entirely, and that we cannot handle it. I just do not buy that idea.[1]

The above remark, made by Chief Judge Harold T. Markey at a conference over twenty-five years ago on science, technology, and judicial decision making, anticipated the turn (after the U.S. Supreme Court issued *Daubert*) toward a more active gatekeeping role for judges with respect to expert scientific testimony. Prior to the *Daubert* Trilogy, federal judges deferred to the scientific community by admitting any expert testimony that reflected "generally accepted" scientific knowledge—a standard that first appeared in *Frye v. United States*, decided by the Federal Court of Appeals in Washington, D.C., in 1923. However, the notion that judges under the earlier *Frye* regime deferred unproblematically to scientists is belied by the proceedings of that 1977 conference, which could easily be mistaken for a contemporary discussion of the problems of how to define science, the distinction between hard and soft science (as well as between scientific and nonscientific expertise), the differences between the legal and scientific enterprises with respect to standards of proof, and the perceived need for science advisors or panels to aid judges in their evaluations of experts. Nevertheless, one recurring theme in the conference, expressed by Chief Judge David L. Bazelon and others, was that judges are not equipped to handle scientific and technical disputes.

> It is hard to imagine a less likely forum for the resolution of technological disputes than our trial courts. Participation in litigation is controlled by the parties who call the witnesses. The information is developed by rules and the strict admission of evidence. The finder of fact, whether it be a judge or a jury, obviously has no claim to expertise in resolving the scientific questions . . . .[2]

Judge Edmund B. Spaeth Jr. agreed that "judges are starting to become very uncomfortable about whether they are being asked to make decisions that really they should not be asked to make because they are not well equipped to make them."[3] That skepticism was echoed (over fifteen years later) by Chief Justice William Rehnquist in *Daubert*, and also by some commentators after *Daubert*.[4] In retrospect, however, Chief Judge Markey's optimism has prevailed:

> We need to develop some understanding of scientists and scientific methods—how they think, how they work, how they arrive at this view and not at that one . . . . I think judges have to learn that scientists do not have two heads. They are not ten feet tall.[5]

An educational, not deferential, model is here suggested for law and science relations.

On the eve of the Supreme Court opinion in *Daubert*, Ronald J. Allen and Joseph S. Miller summarized the ongoing debate over deference or education regarding experts, and tentatively concluded that an education model was preferable if not exclusive.[6] Allen and Miller reformulated a debate between

Ronald Carlson and Paul Rice—over whether the facts or data grounding an expert's opinion should be admissible (Rice) or not (Carlson)[7]—as one over "the extent to which they are willing to defer to experts."[8]

> Carlson's fact finder [i.e., judge or jury] . . . can only attach value to the expert's opinion on the basis of that expert's perceived credibility; the restriction on basis testimony, then, functions to turn the expert into a "super-fact finder capable of producing admissible substantive evidence (an opinion) from inadmissible evidence." Rice prefers that the fact finder be allowed to hear and to use the facts or data that support the expert's opinion to the same extent that the expert uses them.[9]

Professor Rice, in other words, is not as deferential as Professor Carlson. Professor Edward Imwinkelried's position in the debate, building on Judge Learned Hand's suggestion (in 1901) that experts inform the jury of general principles to apply to facts, is strikingly deferential to scientists (though not with respect to the *facts* of a case).[10] Allen and Miller, in response, highlight the problem of conflicting expert testimony, for while the general consensus standard in *Frye* provided a check on jury irrationality (because the jury would be instructed to choose the expert who had the support of the general consensus),

> a system designed to encourage education has considerably less need for such a check, for the check will come from the pedagogical process itself. As the fact finder becomes informed about an area of knowledge, charlatans will be exposed. The Federal Rules thus do not embrace *Frye* [primarily] because they are considerably less dedicated to deference than their common law predecessors. Education is clearly permitted, perhaps encouraged . . . .[11]

Finally, Allen and Miller criticize Richard A. Epstein, who prior to *Daubert* suggested (incorrectly, as it turned out) that the Federal Rules *do* adopt *Frye*'s deferential perspective, as overly deferential to science.[12]

THE TRILOGY OFFERS AN EDUCATIONAL MODEL

Without revisiting the disputes over the proper interpretation of the general acceptance test in *Frye*,[13] we would point out that one of the sensible readings of that opinion would be that judges under the *Frye* regime were to decide two questions, one normative and one empirical. First, the judge would ask whether the witness represented a group worthy to be called scientists (e.g., astrologers, no; chemists, yes). If that normative question could be answered affirmatively, then the empirical question was whether the proffered testimony represented that which was generally accepted in the field. If so, then the judge would *defer* by declaring the testimony admissible.[14] As to what the jury did with that testimony, *Frye* did not address whether the jury was then educated by or deferential to the expert. Trial lawyers presenting such testimony obviously wanted both: a deferential jury that understands and is persuaded by the testimony. Perhaps the judge was exercising a gatekeeping function under *Frye* (by asking the normative and the empirical questions), but the *Daubert* Trilogy confirms that a more aggressive gatekeeping function is now required of judges. *Daubert* held that *Frye* did not survive the Federal Rules,[15] and in *Joiner*, the Supreme Court observed that

> nothing . . . requires a district court to admit opinion evidence which is connected to existing data only by the ipse dixit of the expert. A court may conclude that there is simply too great an analytical gap between the data and the opinion proffered.[16]

That sentence was quoted approvingly in *Kumho Tire*, just after the Court explained that

> no one denies that an expert might draw a conclusion from a set of observations based on extensive and specialized experience. Nor does anyone deny that, as a general matter, tire abuse may often be identified by qualified experts . . . [, but] the question before the trial court was specific, not general . . . [:] whether this particular expert had sufficient specialized knowledge to assist the jurors "in deciding the particular issues in this case."[17]

The best way to read these excerpts, we believe, is as a suggestion that judges should not admit the expert's testimony unless the judge understands its logic, which implies education by the expert as a prerequisite to admissibility, and in recent cases, one can observe an emphasis on the educative role of experts. A short discussion of three recent cases may help the reader get a better feel for what is at stake.

Judges and Juries Need to Understand the Expert

In *Elcock v. Kmart Corporation*, a case involving injuries sustained by a department store patron, the trial judge admitted the testimony of Dr. Chester Copemann, an expert in vocational rehabilitation, and Dr. Bernard Pettingill, an economist. As to Dr. Copemann, the appellate panel held that the trial judge should have held a *Daubert* hearing—an understandable error before *Kumho Tire*—and that "a fuller assessment of Copemann's analytical processes" would have revealed its weaknesses.[18] Specifically, Copemann's methodology in reaching a conclusion of the plaintiff's 50–60 percent disability was neither testable nor reproducible; at best, it was a novel synthesis of two widely used methods, but Copemann "did not demonstrate that this hybrid approach bore a logical relationship to" the established techniques.[19]

> Nor, looking at Copemann's description of his methodology, does it seem that a reasonable explanation could be provided. Given the disconnect between the stated nature of these methods and the results they produced when the facts of the instant case were plugged into the machinery, we hesitate to say that Copemann's method is a reliable one.[20]

Copemann seemed to have made a "subjective judgment . . . in the guise of a reliable expert opinion," which, in *Joiner*'s and *Kumho Tire*'s terminology, was an "ipse dixit statement."[21]

As to Dr. Pettingill, the appellate panel likewise scrutinized his testimony on earning capacity, and found that his conclusions were based on faulty assumptions—for example, that Elcock was 100 percent disabled, that she would have earned twice her pre-injury earnings but for the injury, that she had no post-injury income (she did), and that her life expectancy was average (she had diabetes). In a lengthy footnote exploring the "interstitial gaps among the federal rules," the court explained:

> [A] lost future earnings expert who renders an opinion . . . based on economic assumptions not present in the plaintiff's case cannot be said to "assist the trier of fact," as Rule 702 requires. . . . [Moreover,] it is not a stretch from [Rule 703's] requirement that other "experts in the particular field" would "reasonably rel[y]" on such data in "forming opinions . . . on the subject" . . . to suggest that an expert should not depend on fictional or random data. . . . Rule 402 sets forth a liberal admissibility standard for "[a]ll relevant evidence," defined in Rule 401 as "evidence having any tendency" to make "more probable or less probable" the existence "of any fact . . . of consequence. . . ." Under this framework, an economist's testimony concerning a reliable method for assessing future economic losses can be deemed relevant only insofar as a jury can usefully apply that methodology to the specific facts of a particular plaintiff's case.[22]

Elcock thereby provides an educative model both for judges *applying* the testability standard when conducting a *Daubert* hearing (Copemann's testimony) and for juries *applying* an expert's methodology to the facts (Pettingill's testimony).

Credentials Are Not Enough

In *Goebel v. Denver and Rio Grande Western Railroad Company*, the trial court admitted the testimony of Dr. Daniel T. Teitelbaum, who "purported to establish a causal link between" the plaintiff's cognitive brain damage and his exposure to diesel exhaust in a train tunnel.[23] The defendant on appeal characterized Teitelbaum's testimony as "relying solely upon the *ipse dixit* of the expert"; and because the district court did not hold a *Daubert* hearing to assess Teitelbaum's reasoning and methodology, the appellate panel found an abuse of discretion in admitting the testimony. In short, the trial judge should not have deferred to even a credentialed expert's belief that "on the basis of . . . fundamental physiology," the cognitive defect was caused by exposure to pulmonary irritants at high altitude that produced swelling in the brain. The gatekeeping role required, in various formulations, that trial courts "vigilantly make detailed findings," and that they "carefully and meticulously" review the proffered scientific evidence.[24]

General Acceptance Is Not Enough

Finally, *Libas, Ltd. v. United States*, which reviewed a trial court's determination concerning the weight rather than the admissibility of expert testimony, is significant because it confirms that general acceptance or widespread use—the proxy for reliability under *Frye*'s deferential regime—is not enough to signal reliability under *Daubert*. A key issue at trial was whether a fabric was power-loomed, and the trial judge relied entirely on the results of a Customs Service test that was generally viewed as accurate. The appellate panel held that the trial court should have also taken into account testability, peer-reviewed publication, potential rate of error, or other factors to "assure itself that it has effectively addressed the important issue of reliability. . . ." Once the reliability of a "generally accepted" technique is effectively challenged, as it was by testimony that the fabric came from a village in India with no power looms, a searching analysis is called for.[25]

Together, these cases represent a shift away from deference (to conclusory opinions or "generally accepted" techniques) and toward a pedagogical model for expert testimony—trial judges need to see and understand the logical connections or reasoning leading from principle to application to conclusion, and juries need to apply the experts' methodologies to the facts before them.

THE SOCIAL AUTHORITY OF SCIENCE

What is it, then, that trial judges need to know about science in order to carry out their gatekeeping responsibilities? Several recent federal cases support the notion that trial judges need to be more rigorous in applying the *Daubert* guidelines. In *Ueland v. United States*, for example, a prisoner brought a claim under the Federal Tort Claims Act for back and neck injuries sustained in a collision between a prison van and its "chase car." The plaintiff's principal medical testimony came from "Jason Wilson, a college dropout who claims to be a chiropractor with a practice limited to acupuncture."[26] The judgment in favor of the United States was reversed on several grounds, among them the fact that the

> district judge refused to apply Rule 702 or conduct a *Daubert* inquiry, ruling instead that Wilson's lack of credentials or experience concerns only the weight to be accorded to his testimony. That ruling is wrong. On remand, a *Daubert* inquiry must be conducted, and Wilson's testimony may be received only if . . . [his] "testimony is based upon sufficient facts . . . , the testimony is the product of reliable principles and methods, and . . . the witness has applied the principles and methods reliably . . . ."[27]

Likewise, in *In re Air Crash at Little Rock Arkansas on June 1, 1999*, an airline passenger was awarded damages for injuries sustained during an American Airlines crash. The trial judge admitted the testimony of a Dr. Harris, who testified that the plaintiff's post-traumatic stress disorder was due to a brain dysfunction, but who also "admitted that he did not perform" functional "tests that would have shown physiological changes in the brain" of the plaintiff.[28]

> Unfortunately, the district court does not appear to have considered any of the *Daubert* factors . . . . The district court merely noted that Harris was a qualified psychiatrist, and then stated "It's beyond my competence. I don't know whether . . . there is research material that shows brain changes as a result of the syndrome . . . ." This inquiry was not adequate to satisfy the district court's essential gatekeeping rule under *Daubert*.[29]

Because no tests were performed, "there was no connection established between the alleged physical brain changes" and the plaintiff's condition.[30]

Finally, in *Boncher v. Brown County*, the estate of a prisoner (who committed suicide) brought a section 1983 action against jail officials alleging deliberate indifference to the risk of the prisoner's suicide. The trial judge allowed a criminologist to testify that the number of suicides in the defendant's jail was unusually high, but the appellate panel found that "his evidence was useless and should have been excluded under the *Daubert* standard."[31] Indeed, the expert admitted "that he had neither conducted nor consulted any studies that would have enabled him to compare the [defendant] jail suicide rate with that of the free population or that of other jails."[32] Such cases demonstrate the need for trial judges to be more sophisticated regarding scientific methodology, and perhaps even the need for more judicial training in science, although Judge Richard A. Posner in *Boncher* seized the opportunity in his opinion to educate judges on the concept of normal variance:

> It would not be sound to condemn a jail administrator if the rate of suicide in his population was within one or two standard deviations of the rate elsewhere, for so small a variance might well be due to chance, or at least to factors over which he had no control. Every statistical distribution has an upper tail, and there is no constitutional principle that whoever is unlucky enough to manage the prisons in the upper tail of the distribution of suicides must pay damages.[33]

But a recent decision in *Chapman v. Maytag Corporation* presents an interesting contrast to the above three cases. The trial judge seemed to understand quite clearly that a mechanical engineer's testimony, in support of a wrongful death suit for electrocution by a kitchen range, was less than scientific, but nevertheless the testimony was allowed.[34] According to the appellate panel, the trial judge found that the engineer

> "failed to specify the details supporting his opinion that [the deceased] would have been electrocuted," regardless of whether the outlet was properly grounded. Moreover, the court stated that the lack of any scientific testing presented "a serious problem for the status of [the] testimony as expert opinion."[35]

A new trial was required because "the district court failed to assess whether [the engineer's] theory is scientifically valid,"[36] but the question remained why a judge who seemingly raised the right questions—insufficient details supporting the opinion, lack of any scientific testing—allowed the testimony. Two other recent federal opinions provide a possible answer: the social and institutional, not methodological, authority of science in law sometimes interferes with judicial evaluations of experts.

In *Elsayed Mulchtar v. California State University, Hayward*, a Title VII suit by a professor alleging race discrimination in a denial of tenure, the plaintiff presented Dr. David Wellman as an expert on racism. The trial court admitted Dr. Wellman's testimony "without any discussion of its reliability," and the jury awarded the plaintiff $637,000 in damages. On appeal, in response to the plaintiff's argument that it was a harmless error to admit Dr. Wellman's testimony without a reliability finding (since six of plaintiff's colleagues testified he was qualified for tenure), the university's counsel argued that "Dr. Wellman's testimony was not harmless because it was cloaked in authority. . . ," and that without his testimony, the plaintiff's "evidence could show only [an evenly divided] difference of academic opinion regarding his tenure qualifications."[37] The appellate panel agreed and vacated the judgment—"Dr. Wellman drew the inference of discrimination for the jury, [which] 'more probably than not was the cause of the result reached.'"[38] That notion of being "cloaked in authority," even when there may be no reliability, highlights the potential disconnect between social (or institutional) authority in science and methodological reliability, which the trial judge in *Elsayed Mulchtar* perhaps failed to appreciate.

A similar misunderstanding appeared in *Jinro America Inc. v. Secure Investments, Inc.*, a breach of contract, fraud, and racketeering case in which a purported expert on Korean culture and business practices was allowed to testify. The appellate panel agreed with the plaintiff, who lost at trial, that the expert's "ethnically biased, 'xenophobic' . . . testimony" was "objectionable" and "completely improper." His "sweeping generalizations, derived from his limited experience and knowledge . . . were unreliable and should not have been dignified as expert opinion."[39] But they were, since he

> came before the jury cloaked with the mantle of an expert. This is significant for two reasons. First, it allowed him . . . to couch his observations as generalized "opinions" . . . . Second, his statements were likely to carry special weight with the jury . . . .[40]

We think it is also significant that the appellate panel did not limit their review to the methodological deficiencies—there were many—of the purported expert in *Jinro*, but also discussed a social and institutional aspect of science: its authoritative force, its "cloak" and "mantle" that (due to science's epistemological status) can sometimes get separated from its validity without awareness on the part of the judge or jury. To understand science is to understand that authority is not a natural phenomenon, but a rhetorical accomplishment on the part of those who study nature (and so there are two ways to err). At its best, science represents nature in compelling and useful ways, but to understand science is to recognize that methodological advances can be lost without social authority, as in the case of novel theories that have not yet (but should) gain general acceptance; conversely, methodological mistakes can go unnoticed *because of* social authority, as in the case of *Jinro*.

In *Peabody Coal Company v. McCandless*, the administrative law judge (ALJ) reviewing a Benefits Review Board order in a Black Lung Benefits Act case was faced with conflicting evidence of pneumoconiosis.[41] The pathologist performing the autopsy opined that the miner had pneumoconiosis, but five other physicians disagreed.[42] The ALJ placed "more weight on the opinion of the pathologist who performed the autopsy," but an appellate panel found that decision irrational:

> Although we understand why the ALJ . . . wanted to avoid the medical controversy, . . . [a] scientific dispute must be resolved on scientific grounds, rather than by declaring that whoever examines the cadaver dictates the outcome.[43]

While this outcome on appeal can be explained as an example of a judge who does not understand methodology, it is also an example of how social, institutional, and rhetorical authority gets separated from methodological reliability—if this case had not been appealed, the authority of the pathologist was persuasive enough to establish pneumoconiosis.

The potential disconnect between social authority and methodological reliability is also significant for the debate over whether "legal" science is different from science itself. Because judges are simply not scientists, or because the goals of litigation (e.g., finality) are so different from the goals of practicing scientists (e.g., criticism and refutation), some would argue that "legal" science is not the same as, and never can be, genuine science. Indeed, our arguments about science as a practice to which automatic deference is inappropriate might be viewed as the basis for an appeal to a "legally constructed" science that would coexist alongside "socially constructed" science itself. However, we reject that dichotomy and applaud the trend (in federal courts of appeals) to demand *genuine* science, with all of its own pragmatic limitations, in court.

Recall David Resnik's proposal, discussed in chapter 2, that courts should choose their definition of science on pragmatic grounds, and that their criteria should match the goals and concerns of the courtroom. This formulation implies that science's own standards of validity should be different from legal standards of scientific validity. Brian Leiter takes this position in his critique of Heidi Feldman's argument that *Daubert* appropriately adopted a revised empiricist philosophy of science (thereby bringing law into line with actual scientific practice).[44] For Leiter, there is "no reason to think admissibility standards ought to conform" to the "dominant, or even the correct, philosophy of science."

> Courtrooms, after all, are not laboratories, and judges are not scientists . . . . The rules of evidence serve [not only the discovery of truth but also] the promotion of various policy objectives . . . and the efficient and timely resolution of disputes.
>
> * * * *
>
> We plainly want our science in the courtroom to bear some relation to real science . . . . But this goal must be pursued in light of the serious epistemic limits of courts—intellectual, temporal, material.[45]

Admissibility questions are, for Leiter, questions of social epistemology: "under the real-world epistemic limits of a particular social process for the acquisition of knowledge, what epistemic norms actually work the best?"[46]

Leiter's style of pragmatism, which inevitably presumes that there is some *real* laboratory science that never quite makes it into court, is not the pragmatism we identified among federal appellate judges. Rather, their view of *real* science itself as already a pragmatic practice — perhaps a minor devaluation of science — is combined with an educational model of what scientists do in court to create an *actual* scientific discourse in law. In effect, for these judges, science is not as complex, and courts are not as limited, as Leiter suggests. Indeed, if scientific knowledge is always approximate and probabilistic, it is not so different from law. Science too, in Leiter's terminology, has serious "intellectual, temporal, [and] material" epistemic limitations.[47] While some education is necessary, and some translation warranted, the standards for science in law should mirror the standards for scientists generally. Courts therefore generously cite Chief Judge Posner's requirement "that when scientists testify in court they adhere to the same standards of intellectual rigor that are demanded in their professional work."[48]

OVERCOMING THE METHODOLOGICAL VERSUS SOCIAL DICHOTOMY IN LAW

In any truly public battle, those arguing for constructivism in general will lose to those arguing for reality in general. What is necessary is first an at least rhetorical concession to the power of the argument for reality, and second, a demonstration of the way particular uses of the constructivist position are humanly helpful and consistent with a rigorous science.[49]

While we will not attempt in this chapter to introduce or revisit the polarizing debates about the role of social interests in the production of scientific knowledge, it is important to acknowledge that those debates keep many historians, philosophers, and sociologists of science busy. In the science wars, the "rational and the social are dichotomized and the debate is about which ought to be given primacy in accounting for scientific knowledge."[50] Sociologists of science, for example, identify and emphasize "the practices and processes that . . . succeed in ratifying some content . . . as knowledge in a given community," whereby science is "a process of developing . . . new accounts of natural processes in such a way as to effect general assent to those accounts."[51] Unfortunately, that emphasis seems to destabilize or undermine science as a reliable source of knowledge because of an overt dependency on "community" or "general assent." Scientific representations, we might say, should be *caused* by nature or reality, not by communal assent, and certainly not by rhetorical techniques. A scientist's account might therefore emphasize the processes and practices that justify knowledge "independently of community practices."

One can speak of the knowledge of an individual as the intersection of what the individual believes (justifiably) and the set of all truths [e.g., concerning nature], or the knowledge of a community as the intersection of what is accepted (justifiably, or as a consequence of normatively sanctioned practices) by a community with the set of all truths.[52]

Unfortunately again, that emphasis on truth seems to idealize science by ignoring the historical evolution of scientific knowledge as well as the social, institutional, and rhetorical aspects of justification and "normatively sanctioned practices."

Numerous theorists have therefore concluded that the choice between a view of science as fundamentally social (or cultural) or as fundamentally rational (or methodological) is a false dualism. Helen Longino, for example, concedes that justification is contextual, but need not be arbitrary or subjective, since it is

dependent on rules and procedures immanent in the context of inquiry. Contextualism is the nondichotomist's alternative to [sociological] relativism and [rationalistic] absolutism regarding justification.[53]

Bruno Latour likewise argues that "scientific facts are indeed constructed, but they cannot be reduced to the social dimension"—networks of scientific knowledge are "*simultaneously real, like nature, narrated, like discourse, and collective, like society* . . . ."[54] In another formulation, Slavoj Zizek asks:

[I]s historicist relativism (which ultimately leads to the untenable solipsist position) really the only alternative to naive realism (according to which, in the sciences . . . , we are gradually approaching the proper image of the way things are out there, independently of our consciousness of them)?[55]

What is missed in that dichotomy, Zizek suggests, was indicated by Thomas Kuhn when

he claimed that the shift in a scientific paradigm is MORE than a mere shift in our (external) perception on/perception of reality, but nonetheless LESS than our effectively "creating" another new reality.[56]

While such notions are complex and sometimes counterintuitive—hence the tendency toward false dichotomies—they are particularly useful in explaining some of the confusion in *Daubert* Trilogy jurisprudence. The inevitable social, institutional, and rhetorical aspects of science are not the opposite of scientific methodology, but its context.

In our analysis of federal appellate court opinions, we identified various instances where trial judges did not appreciate the social, institutional, and rhetorical aspects of science. In reversing district court admissibility decisions, the appellate panels identified the social authority of scientists that can interfere with methodological evaluations, as well as the pragmatic limitations on science that arise because not all hypotheses are the subject of well-established standards, past research interests, or extensive testing. The mantle of authority is not a marker of reliability, but neither are the pragmatic limitations on science markers of unreliability. Science is a network of communities, institutions, persuasion, and consensus-building; methodological norms can sometimes provide a check on these features, but such norms are also part of the network.

Relying primarily on recent federal appellate opinions that reversed trial judges' evaluations of admissibility of scientific evidence, chapter 2 and this chapter highlight three tendencies in the wake of *Daubert*: (i) a pragmatist orientation with respect to ongoing philosophical disputes concerning the nature and reliability of the scientific enterprise; (ii) an orientation to an educational, rather than a deferential, model of the relationship between science and gatekeeping judges; and (iii) a merger of legal and scientific discourse, that is, a tendency to resist the notion that, in determinations of validity, law and science operate on justifiably different grounds. We conclude that these trends ought to lead away from false dichotomies between nature and culture, between methodology and social context, and even between genuine and junk science when experts disagree.

> When facts are in dispute, experts sometimes reach different conclusions based on competing versions of the facts. The emphasis in [Rule 702] on "sufficient facts or data" is not intended to authorize a trial court to exclude an expert's testimony on the ground that the court believes one version of the facts and not the other.[57]

While the foregoing might seem obvious, the court of appeals in *Pipitone* viewed the trial court's exclusion of plaintiff's infectious disease expert as "the precise problem" identified above.[58] Perhaps there is a tendency in law to see every dispute as having two sides, only one of which will win. Perhaps it is a scientistic culture, and not a legal culture, that is responsible for the sense that when two scientific experts disagree, one of them must be unreliable. Scientific debate, however, can

> be understood as an ongoing process of critical interaction that both prevents closure where it is inappropriate and helps to establish limits of (relative) certainty . . . .
>
> [I]t makes no sense to detach measurements and data descriptions from the contexts in which they are generated . . . . [A]s soon as one does, one creates a new context relative to which they are to be assessed and understood.[59]

However, the sense in scientistic culture that contexts are unstable leads some consumers of science, including trial judges, to want more than social authority, institutional gatekeeping, and rhetorical ornaments—they want reality. Indeed, that distinction between context and reality gives the social, institutional, and rhetorical features of science a pejorative connotation. Science should, one might say, represent nature and not funding interests, lofty credentials, communal assent, or good argumentative techniques. The same distinction, a false dualism, has made its way into training manuals for attorneys who cross-examine experts, with the result that bias, interests, and motivations are seen as bad, which implies that genuine expertise is unbiased, disinterested, and unmotivated. While it is true that some experts may be biased toward a pet theory, financially invested in their client's cause, or motivated by greed, the very notion of disembodied, detached, and noncontextual science is the product of an unjustified dichotomy. Fidelity on the part of scientists to contemporary methodological conventions *is* a bias, an interest, and a motivation—but that is what we want. Moreover, involvement on the part of scientists in the social networks of their profession can help them generate reliable science—and that is also what we want.

Having looked in the last two chapters at how judges idealize science, which idealization alternatively results in excessive skepticism (toward good scientists) and excessive deference (even toward bad scientists), we turn to the discourse among legal scholars who specialize in scientific evidence. Unfortunately, just as judges are tempted to idealize science, many scholars tend to fall prey to a similar idealization.

NOTES

1. Remarks by Chief Judge Harold T. Markey, U.S. Court of Customs and Patent Appeals, in *Science, Technology and Judicial Decision-Making: An Exploratory Discussion* (proceedings of a conference on the subject held in September 1977) (ed. J. D. Nyhart, 1981), at 12.

2. *See id.* at 14 (remarks by Chief Judge David L. Bazelon).

3. *See id.* at 17 (remarks by Judge Edmund Spaeth).

4. *See Daubert*, 509, U.S. at 600 (Rehnquist, C. J., concurring in part and dissenting in part); *see also* Brian Leiter, "The Epistemology of Admissibility: Why Even Good Philosophy of Science Would Not Make for Good Philosophy of Evidence," 1997 *B.Y.U. L. Rev.* 803.

5. *See* Markey, *supra* note 1, at 12.

6. *See* Ronald J. Allen and Joseph S. Miller, "The Common Law Theory of Experts: Deference or Education?" 87 *Nw. U. L. Rev.* 1131, 1137 (1993).

7. In other words, should the jury hear only the expert's opinion, or should the jury also hear the data (which is probably hearsay) that the expert used in generating the opinion?

8. *See id.* at 1136, citing Ronald L. Carlson, "Policing the Bases of Modern Expert Testimony," 39 *Vand. L. Rev.* 577 (1986); Paul Rice, "Inadmissible Evidence as a Basis for Expert Opinion Testimony: A Response to Professor Carlson," 40 *Vand. L. Rev.* 583 (1987).

9. Allen and Miller, *supra* note 6, at 1135.

10. See Edward J. Imwinkelried, "The 'Bases' of Expert Testimony: The Syllogistic Structure of Scientific Testimony," 67 *N.C. L. Rev.* 1 (1988).

11. *See* Allen and Miller, *supra* note 6, at 1140, 1142.

12. *See id.* at 1142–46, citing Richard Epstein, "A New Regime for Expert Witnesses," 26 *Val. U. L. Rev.* 757, 758–60 (1992); *see also* Richard A. Epstein, "Judicial Control over Expert Testimony: Of Deference and Education," 87 *Nw. U. L. Rev.* 1156, 1158 (1993). "Learned opinion is divided on the subject [of the status of *Frye* under the Rules of Evidence]." *Id.* at 1158 n.9.

13. *See* 293 F. 1013, 1014 (D.C. Cir. 1923) (scientific principle "from which the deduction is made must be sufficiently established to have gained general acceptance in the particular field in which it belongs").

14. As others have pointed out, the *Frye* test (which is still used in many states) has developed in recent decades into numerous tests, some of which are less deferential and involve more scrutiny of an expert's testimony. *See generally* David E. Bernstein, "*Frye, Frye,* Again: The Past, Present, and Future of the General Acceptance Test," 41 *Jurimetrics* 385, 386–87 (2001) ("Many jurisdictions continue to adhere to *Frye* . . . ."); *see also id.* at 388 ("case law under *Frye* is slowly converging with *Daubert* jurisprudence"), 393 ("Courts in *Frye* jurisdictions are beginning to . . . hold that an expert's methodology *and* reasoning should be scrutinized"), 404 ("*Frye* courts are stretching *Frye* beyond its original boundaries in a struggle to keep up with Supreme Court precedents"). Consequently, it is improper either to refer to *Frye* as outdated or to view its general acceptance test as somehow fixed. *See* Note, "*Frye* Versus *Daubert*: Practically the Same?" 87 *Minn. L. Rev.* 1579, 1580–81.

Although states vary widely in how they treat certain types of scientific evidence, this variation does not correlate with the adherence to *Frye* or *Daubert* admissibility standards. The inherent breadth . . . of the inquiries compatible with either standard permits widely variable opinions concerning admissibility of a single scientific methodology.

Id. at 1619.

15. *See* 509 U.S. at 589.

16. *See Joiner,* 522 U.S. at 146.

17. *See Kumho Tire,* 526 U.S. at 156, quoting 4 J. McLaughlin, *Weinstein's Federal Evidence* para. *702.05[1],* at 702–33 (2d ed. 1992).

18. 233 F.3d 734, 744–45 (3rd Cir. 2000).

19. *See* 233 F.3d at 747–48.

20. *See* 233 F.3d at 750.

21. *See* 233 F.3d at 747, 748.

22. *See* 233 F.3d at 755–56 and 756 n. 13.

23. 215 F.3d 1083, 1085 (10th Cir. 2000).

24. *See* 215 F.3d at 1086–8.

25. *See* 193 F.3d 1361, 1365–7 (Fed. Cir. 1999).

Here, where Libas effectively challenged the reliability of the Customs procedure, the trial court should have examined the Customs test either with a *Daubert*-style analysis or in some other equally searching way.

Id. at 1368.

26. 291 F.3d 993, 994, 997 (7th Cir. 2002).

27. *Id.*, citing *Fed. R. Evid.* 702.

28. 291 F.3d 503, 508, 513 (8th Cir. 2002).

29. 291 F.3d at 514.

30. *See id.* Dr. Harris "based his conclusion on Lloyd's disrupted sleep, lack of concentration and flashbacks. This was an inadequate foundation upon which to base the opinion that a *physical change* had taken place in Lloyd's brain." *Id.* at 514–15.

31. 272 F.3d 484, 485–86 (7th Cir. 2001).

32. *See* 272 F.3d at 487. Note that the appellate panel affirmed the summary judgment in favor of the defendant; we include this case as an example of a rejection of a trial judge's admissibility decision notwithstanding affirmance of the trial court's judgment.

33. *See* 272 F.3d at 487.

34. 297 F.3d 682, 686 (7th Cir. 2002).

35. *See* 297 F.3d at 686.

36. *See id.*

37. 299 F.3d at 1053, 1061, 1064, 1067 (9th Cir. 2002).

38. 299 F.3d at 1068, quoting *Jauregui v. City of Glendale*, 852 F.2d 1128, 1133 (9th Cir. 1988).

39. 266 F.3d 993, 996, 1006 (9th Cir. 2000).

40. 266 F.3d at 1004.

41. 255 F.3d 465, 467 (7th Cir. 2001).

42. *Id.* "One of these . . . added that [the] analysis of [the pathologist performing the autopsy] depended on views expressed in a 1981 article that had been discredited in the medical literature, and that as a result [the pathologist's] conclusion is worthless." *Id.*

43. 255 F.3d at 468 ("junk science cannot be rescued by some principle such as a doctrine that courts must receive the views of any expert who does hands-on work").

44. *See* Leiter, *supra* note 4, at 805, referring to Heidi Feldman, "Science and Uncertainty," 74 *Texas L. Rev.* 1 (1995).

45. *See* Leiter, *supra* note 4, at 805, 816.

46. *See id.* at 814.

47. *See id.* at 817.

48. *See Rosen v. Ciba-Geigy Corp.*, 78 F.3d 316, 318 (7th Cir. 1986). A Lexis search turned up hundreds of federal cases using this phrase, including *Kumho Tire*, 526 U.S. at 152 (where Justice Stephen Breyer used Judge Richard Posner's formulation without a formal citation, which suggests that Posner's suggestion is on its way to becoming the sort of common sense that needs no citation).

49. George Levine, "What Is Science Studies for and Who Cares?" 46–47 *Social Text* 113, 126 (1996).

50. *See* Helen E. Longino, *The Fate of Knowledge* 77 (2002).

51. *See id.* at 78–79.

52. *See id.* at 83–84.

53. *See id.* at 92.

54. *See* Bruno Latour, *We have Never Been Modern* 6 (trans. Catherine Porter, 1993).

55. *See* Slavoj Zizek, "Lacan between Cultural Studies and Cognitivism," in *Lacan and Science* (ed. J. Glynos and Y. Stavrakis, 2002), at 299.

56. *See id.* at 300.

57. Advisory Committee notes, *Fed. R. Evid.* 702.

58. *See Pipitone*, 288 F.3d at 249.

59. *See* Longino, *supra* note 50, at 177, 201.

Chapter Four

The Idealizations of Legal Scholars

AT A GATHERING OF EVIDENCE PROFESSORS

The public mind [in 1850s New Orleans] is bewildered by the contradictory opinions given by the Engineers in the state as to what ought and ought not to be done. One says cut-offs is the only means of protecting the country. Another says cut-offs will ruin the country [so] make levees only . . . . A third says make outlets. Each one quotes opinions of foreign engineers and partial facts and pretended facts respecting the Mississippi [River] to support his views. No wonder the legislature does nothing.[1]

In 2003, on the occasion of the tenth anniversary of *Daubert v. Merrell Dow Pharmaceuticals, Inc.*, Seton Hall University School of Law held a symposium titled "Expert Admissibility: Keeping Gates, Goals and Promises" [hereinafter Seton Hall Symposium]. The *Seton Hall Law Review* published the symposium's proceedings in two issues, wherein numerous leading evidence scholars, as well as practitioners and a judge, discussed the jurisprudence of scientific experts.[2] Given the flurry of scholarship that arose immediately following *Daubert* and the other two important opinions (*General Electric Co. v. Joiner* and *Kumho Tire Co., Ltd. v. Carmichael*)[3] that along with *Daubert* comprise the *Daubert* Trilogy, one might have expected the Seton Hall Symposium to be a celebration of clarity and progress. This expectation, however, went unmet. Rather than bringing clarity, *Daubert* has spawned a series of intense debates and controversies concerning the types of evidence that are, should be, or should not be admissible in court, the role of judges and juries regarding expertise, and needed reforms.

As explained in chapter 1, the *Daubert* Trilogy deflects attention away from abstract identifications of scientific validity, including the "demarcation" controversy concerning the elimination of alleged junk science from the

49

courtroom. Instead, attention is directed toward the application of expertise to the particular case at hand. This emphasis on application was reflected as well in the Seton Hall Symposium proceedings, although many participants failed to remain oriented to the problem of application. Nevertheless, at their best, the authors attended to the right issues. First, there was a pragmatic recognition, in various forms, that the focus should be on how science is being used rather than on science in the abstract. Second, there was the recognition that the focus must be accompanied by a modest view of science rather than an idealized version of its capacity to produce knowledge for law. Third, there was an awareness that the focus on the application phase of expertise must also be accompanied by a modest view of law itself, including trial judges, lawyers, juries, and the appellate judiciary. It is far too easy to romanticize the power of science, or the virtues of the legal system, or both, and to fail to recognize their practical limitations. Just as romantic images of law often rely on the demonization of judges untrained in science, of overzealous lawyers, or of emotional, uncritical, and confused jurors, romantic images of science are often bolstered by demonization of forensic scientists, plaintiffs' experts, or social science. Thus, the pragmatic emphasis on application must be mediated by pragmatic views of both science and law. Fortunately, the pragmatic aspects of science and law—which we associate with their local, social, rhetorical, and institutional features—are most visible in the focus on application. Nevertheless, at the Seton Hall Symposium, the limitations of law and science often receded into the background, and as a result, undue attention was given to red herrings and unrealistic reform proposals. Since the symposium was a mixed bag of error and insight, we believe that a careful review may give the reader a more detailed understanding of how to think about the intersection of science and law. We acknowledge that a debate among legal academics lacks any intrinsic interest to anyone who is sane, so we shall not report the details of the combat. We shall try to abstract out the substance, which we think is both important and interesting.

Further, we are confident that the substance of the debate will interest any scholar who studies the policy-making process in administrative agencies and legislatures. In this chapter, therefore, we also discuss academic proposals to reform the way that judges, jurors, and lawyers use science. We think that proposed reforms for the way science is used by administrative agencies and legislatures will raise many of the same issues.

THE ACTION IS IN THE APPLICATION

[T]he answer to what question is to be asked of the expert post-*Kumho* is precisely whatever questions should have been asked post- (and for that matter pre-) *Daubert*, to-wit: Does the expert in fact possess knowledge useful to this trial that is being brought to bear upon it in a way that increases the probability of accurate outcomes?[4]

The proper emphasis on application in determining the admissibility of expert testimony is epitomized in the phrase "brought to bear." One must focus on the way science is used in the courtroom, not on science or law in the abstract. Otherwise there is a risk, in post-*Daubert* legal discourse, that one's scholarly analysis or reform proposal will "smell of the lamp" and be of no use in the rather rough arena that is a trial—that which looks elegant and symmetrical in the study can look deformed in the courtroom.

In contemporary, post-*Daubert* discourse, the focus on application takes numerous forms. For example, Professors Samuel Gross and Jennifer Mnookin, after noting that "thousands of pages have been written about both the proper [threshold] criteria for evaluating the reliability of expert evidence and the institutional competence of judges to evaluate scientific reliability," recommend that we examine "another dimension: the degree of certainty that the expert posits in what she offers."[5]

> One of the central problems with much expert testimony introduced in court— both scientific and non-scientific alike—is that experts claim as matters of fact or probability opinions that should be couched in more cautious terms, as pos- sibilities or hypotheses.
>   . . . Often, whether testimony is based on scientific study or more casual forms of observation, what makes an expert's conclusion unreliable is that it is expressed with a confidence not warranted by the evidence.[6]

Moreover, even some scholars who disagree over whether *Daubert* as applied is too restrictive or not restrictive enough agree on the need to focus on the application phase. For example, Professor Michael Saks, who is concerned that the value of much forensic science continues to be exaggerated, summa- rizes the elemental conditions of admissibility of expert evidence as follows: "(a) the opinions and conclusions of the expert are accompanied by informa- tion that enables the factfinder to evaluate the likely accuracy of the expert's opinion, and (b) the information is presented in such a way that factfinders will not . . . excessively [overvalue] the testimony."[7] Likewise, Professor Richard Friedman—who, in contrast with Professor Saks, criticizes the *Daubert* regime as overly exclusionary—nevertheless recommends that "in some settings . . . courts should admit expert evidence but explain to the jury factors limiting the weight that the jury should accord the evidence . . . . Sometimes the . . . court[s] should . . . comment adversely on it."[8] Therefore, reliability in the abstract may not be as important as whether "the expert wit- ness over-claimed the significance" of the result of forensic scientific inquiry.[9]

All of these variable expositions on confidence levels—the manner in which evidence is used, and whether experts overclaim or juries overvalue it—emphasize the application phase of expertise.

Assuming that one focuses on how science is "brought to bear" in the courtroom, and that one takes a modest and non-romantic view of both law and science, what are the principal problems and greatest dangers that we face? Where could improvements be made that will lead to more accurate decisions? With these questions in mind, several suggestions made during the Seton Hall Symposium appear promising. For example, Professor Dale Nance observed that current "practice is often overly generous to proponents in allowing opinion on case-specific material facts . . . , when those facts are not within the personal knowledge of the expert."[10] With respect to fingerprint identification expertise, Professor Saks confirmed that

> a court must determine what the fingerprint comparison problem is (a clear and complete latent print versus a tiny fragment versus a montage of numerous overlaid smeared latents, etc.) and whether the data show that the expert is likely to be able to perform that particular type of examination accurately. Under [*Kumho Tire*], a court is not to ask about a field in a general and global way.[11]

Hence, the recommendation by some scholars that "[j]udicial comment, expressing reasons to limit the significance of the evidence, [is sometimes] appropriate."[12]

To be sure, the task of improving the way in which science is brought to bear is not trivial. Rather, it is worth our best efforts to generate creative suggestions to aid the bench and bar in the application phase of expertise in the courtroom. Many scholars, in criticizing existing practices and in their proposals for reform, acknowledge the significance of the application phase. Nevertheless, many still fail to possess modest expectations of both science and law. Too many academics idealize either law or science—respectively demonizing, on the one hand, courtroom experts, and on the other hand, judges, lawyers, and juries. Given that both law and science are local and cultural enterprises with practical goals and limitations, a non-romantic, pragmatic approach to both is appropriate.

Idealizing law or science prevents one from focusing on the most important problem associated with the use of science (and other evidence) at trials. Our own view of the matter accords with that expressed in *Schafersman v. Agland Cooperative*, where the Nebraska Supreme Court stated that they were

> convinced that by shifting the focus to the kind of reasoning required in science—empirically supported rational explanations—the *Daubert/Joiner/Kumho*

Tire trilogy of cases greatly improves the reliability of the information upon which verdicts and other legal decisions are based. Because courts and juries cannot do justice in a factual vacuum, the better information the fact finders have, the more likely that verdicts will be just.[13]

What we like most about this statement, brought to our attention by Professor Joseph Sanders,[14] is its definition of the scientific method as "empirically supported rational explanations." Notably, this form of reasoning should also be at the core of law, journalism, history, sociology, and any other form of thought that, however distant the support and uncertain the conclusions, purports to base conclusions on facts.[15] This sort of modest, realistic assessment of what science (and law) should hope to achieve is the only plausible way to identify the true problems that arise from the use of scientific evidence in court. Conversely, idealistic pictures of law and science stand in the way of understanding the real problems.

Furthermore, abstract theorizing about what science is does not seem profitable. After all, law professors, lawyers, and judges have a rather remote chance of successfully identifying a set of useful and cogent criteria that would demark science from nonscience.[16] As noted above, we do not think that Justice Harry Blackmun intended to construct a definition of science; furthermore, the crucial precedents do not seem to turn on that inquiry. For example, in *Daubert* on remand, *Joiner*, and *Kumho Tire*, the judges never stated that the excluded testimony was the product of junk science. In each of these cases, the judges accepted that the field of expertise that formed the basis of the excluded testimony was wholly legitimate.[17] On the other hand, in each of these cases, the judges determined that the application of the expertise, that is, the way in which the expertise was brought to bear, was dubious.

In the next section, we begin by identifying some idealizations of science in recent post-*Daubert* scholarship. In our analysis of each, we explore the manner in which romantic images of science deflect attention away from the application phase, resulting in proposals for reform that are unworkable. Along the way, we also set forth the contours of a modest view of science.

MODEST VERSUS IDEALIZED VIEWS OF SCIENCE

The closer the empirical focus on the actual workings of science, and the more current and uncertain the area of science examined, the more difficult it is to identify simple ideal models of methods and norms.[18]

Certain idealizations of science are easier to detect than others. To be sure, it is difficult, in light of scientific progress, to locate persons who view science as merely a social or cultural phenomenon not unlike religion or mythology. Similarly, it is not easy to find persons who view the scientific enterprise as simply an accumulated body of objective, universal, timeless truths. Nevertheless, between those extremes, judges and commentators may expect too much from science in the courtroom. The basis of such expectations is often a subtle idealization of the scientific enterprise. Although science is best characterized by both (i) its methodological rigor and technically efficacious outcomes, and (ii) its social, institutional, and rhetorical features, an undue focus on the former characteristics can deflect attention away from the latter.

Michael Baumeister and Dorothea Capone's account of post-*Daubert* expertise, for example, begins with a modest view of science in law, seeing it as probabilistic, sometimes shaky, and often uncertain.[19] Their essential argument, that toxic tort plaintiffs are unfairly disadvantaged by post-*Daubert* reliability requirements, concludes by drawing an analogy between plaintiffs' experts and Copernicus, whose novel "theories and research [might not] find their way past the admissibility gates of an increasingly imperial judiciary applying a *Daubert* analysis."[20]

> Early in the sixteenth century, great thinkers of the Western World unanimously believed that the earth lay at the center of the universe . . . . So deeply held was this belief, that it was considered heresy to think otherwise. But one man dared to believe otherwise. Nicolaus Copernicus, sitting alone in a turret and using just his eyes . . . sketched and re-sketched his celestial observations.[21]

This romantic picture, offered with citations to an *Irish Times* article and two Web sites,[22] represents science as the product of an individual standing alone against the community; the role of social institutions is either negative or nonexistent. In this story, the social aspects of science belong to the mainstream scientific community, where strong commitments, leaps of faith, omission of counterarguments, political strategies, and religious devotion hinder scientific discovery and progress. However, Copernicus was not alone, did not use only *his* eyes, had strong commitments, engaged in leaps of faith, omitted counterarguments, and was both politically astute and religious.[23] The analogy breaks down because the social, institutional, and rhetorical aspects of science are not simply impediments to overcome; inevitably, they are aspects of good science. That is, they make the best science possible. Naturally in certain cases, social factors—such as fraud due to ambition, laboratory carelessness, and refusal to acknowledge data that contradict a favored theory—serve as barriers to scientific progress. Nevertheless, the *social* is a feature of both science's failures and science's successes. Significantly, scientific progress relies on social interaction, institutional support, and rhetorical strategies, including consensus-building techniques, persuasion, and governing metaphors and models.

Other idealizations of science are more difficult to detect, especially when they come in the form of an empirical description of our state of affairs following *Daubert*. (At this point, we step away from the Seton Hall Symposium to a social-science study that may have influenced some of the symposium's authors.)

Evaluating Judicial Knowledge of Science

Survey results demonstrate that . . . many of the judges surveyed lacked the scientific literacy seemingly necessitated by *Daubert*.[24]

The passage we have just quoted comes from an article in which six social scientists start with the right question, "What do judges, and the rest of us, need to know about science?" and end up with the wrong answer. One should note how stark their conclusions are:

One-third of the judges surveyed . . . believed that the intent of *Daubert* was to raise the threshold of admissibility, whereas 23% . . . believed that the intent was to lower the threshold . . . . Just over one-third . . . believed the intent was to neither raise nor lower the threshold . . . . The remaining judges (11% . . .) were uncertain as to the Supreme Court's intention.[25]

As to science itself, the same survey indicated that most judges lack a clear understanding of falsifiability and error rate, leading its authors to conclude that judges "need to be trained to be critical consumers of the science that comes before them."[26]

The authors of this survey depicted a striking picture of confusion in the wake of *Daubert*. The blame, according to the survey authors, lies partly with the *Daubert* opinion (and the Court's failure to provide guidance as to the gatekeeping role), and partly with judges who generally lack scientific literacy.[27] Offering scientific training for judges impliedly solves both problems since an understanding of science makes the *Daubert* guidelines clear (assuming the *Daubert* guidelines represent science).

From the perspective of those who do fieldwork in the public understanding of science, this recent survey is typical of the deficit model in traditional, *quantitative* studies.[28] Science is presumed, in such research, to be secure and measurable knowledge that an unknowledgeable public lacks and needs, the remedy being usually conceived to be more science education, which conception reinvokes the image of cognitive content to be delivered into a repository characterized by its social or communal features.[29] More recent interpretationist, *qualitative* fieldwork indicates that the public "uptake" of science involves two communities: (i) the scientific enterprise, and (ii) the local public being advised—each of which possesses "socially grounded, conditional, and value-laden" knowledge.[30] The public, these studies have shown, are not simply unknowledgeable, but are also suspicious of the interests of scientists, and aware of scientific controversies, inconsistencies, and errors.[31] This critically reflective model of the public understanding of science is an attempt to identify the social relations of trust and credibility that affect the public reception of scientific knowledge. Judges not trained in science who are used to seeing experts disagree are more like the public than like amateur scientists, and their relationship with science is more complex than the deficit model, exemplified in the recent survey, suggests.

How does one determine what judges are doing with the *Daubert* Trilogy? And how does one assess how well they are doing it? Of course, the second question (evaluation) cannot be asked until the first one is answered, and so it is sensible to begin with trying to find out the empirical facts, namely, what are the judges doing? Finding such facts is not easy, but scholars have a duty to inquire, and to attempt to discover what is happening. The six scholars who reported their findings in "Asking the Gatekeepers" (see note 24) decided to find the empirical facts of the matter by asking judges what they do. In the course of this chapter, we will continue to be highly critical of that study—we think that in the course of their fieldwork, the six scholars asked judges the wrong questions, and furthermore, we think that the basic methodology of their survey was flawed. Yet even though we are critical, we think that the study is important, since we also think that the views of the six authors represent an important position, and one that has some social power. And since we think those powerful views are erroneous, we wish to take them seriously.

In order to ask judges what they are doing, one must proceed in a systematic way, and the six scholars that we wish to confront certainly satisfy the requirement of proceeding systematically. They describe their methodology with admirable clarity. First, they used standard sources to generate a representative sample of the judiciary. Their sample is what statisticians would call a "stratified random sample," and we agree that using a stratified sample, rather than a simpler sampling technique, was the correct way to proceed. As the authors state, by using a stratified sample they were able to ensure that their sample was "representative of [both] geographic distribution of judges and levels of court."[32]

The six scholars also pretested their survey instrument, which is a standard precaution. They tried it out on focus groups of judges who were attending classes at the National Judicial College through its Judicial Studies Program. As it turns out, this preliminary version of the survey ruffled the feathers of the judges, since they thought they were being tested. Of course, the judicial reaction was accurate—the whole point of the survey was to test how well judges understood their job. On the face of the survey, it was a simple empirical inquiry; but a fair reading of the article will reveal that the six do not wish merely to report on what judges are doing; they also wish to evaluate judicial performance. However, discretion is often wise, and so the six revised their survey questions so as to make them more diplomatic.

The next step was to try to get the sample of judges to cooperate. To do this, the six scholars proceeded in a sensible way. They sent out an introductory letter that was followed up by a phone call. In the phone call, the scholars' intent was to persuade the judges to participate in an interview, and then, if that persuasion was successful, to schedule an interview. For the most part, it appears that the persuasion and the scheduling went well.

The tricky part of the process was to teach interviewers how to ask the questions and how to code the answers. Asking the questions was no simple matter. Of necessity, the questions were open-ended, and so the interviewers had a difficult task. Depending on what the answer was, there were different sorts of follow-up questions that would be appropriate. We recognize that it would be extremely difficult to execute well the complicated agenda that the six scholars set for themselves in the conduct of the interviews and the coding of the answers, and we do not wish to quibble about administrative details. We are quite confident that we could do no better. Our criticism of their study does not go to the technical details of administration. We wish to criticize the questions they asked of the judges, not the details of how well they asked those questions.

The question that the six scholars address in their survey is "How well do judges understand the *Daubert* criteria?" Since two of the four *Daubert* criteria, peer review and general acceptance, do not cause anyone any problems, the survey reduces to the question "Do judges understand the concepts of falsifiability and error rate?" Since we think that there is a subtle but important error here, let us quote a key passage from the article.

> In order [for a judge's responses] to be coded as "judge understands concept" for any *Daubert* criterion, the judge had to refer to the central scientific meaning of the concept. For example, with respect to falsifiability, in order for a response to be coded as "judge understands concept," the judge's response had to make explicit reference to testability, test and disproof, prove wrong a theory or hypothesis, or proof/disproof.[33]

On the face of the matter, perhaps nothing seems radically wrong with this quotation, but we wish to argue that the six scholars are proceeding in the wrong way. To begin, one should note that the project proceeds on the assumption that there is such a thing as "the central scientific meaning" of the relevant concepts, which seems to us a highly oversimplified view of science. While scientists do adhere to the ideal of falsifiability, the actual concrete meaning of this difficult concept varies across time and across disciplines.[34] As we understand it, no scientist would argue that falsifiability is not a crucial concept, and yet one can observe (if one only looks) that scientists disagree vehemently at times about whether a particular hypothesis has or has not been falsified.

The next point to make is that the six scholars are proceeding on the assumption that the judges somehow lack essential knowledge if they do not understand the concept of falsifiability the way that the six scholars understand it. Again, we refer to this assumption as the deficit model. Those who believe in the deficit model postulate an ideal science, and all nonscientists are assumed to be defective to the degree that they do not understand this scientific ideal. But how can one be defective for not understanding an ideal concept if the actual practice of science departs from the idealistic norm?[35] As we have already pointed out, when one looks at the actual practice of science, one sees profound disagreements over whether particular hypotheses have or have not been falsified. Is this evidence that scientists themselves understand the concept in different ways?

We imagine that the six scholars might respond to these two criticisms in ways that many will find cogent. For example, they might say, "We six understand that the concept of falsifiability is applied in different ways, but the concept itself is not meaningless, even when it is abstract." Assuming that they would say something like this, we willingly agree. Then they might continue by saying, "And we six think that we have captured the abstract meaning of the concept." Once again, we are happy to agree. But notice where this leaves the debate. All agree on the abstract meaning of the concept (which the six capture reasonably well). The disagreement is in its application. If this is a fair statement of the matter, then one must notice that the real work is being done at the moment when the concept is applied. And if the real work is done when the concept is applied, then one must face the following question: "Are all applications of the concept equally good?" We will assume that we and the six would agree on a negative answer to this question. Some scientists are better than others; some apply the concept of falsifiability with more insight that others do.

If the reader can agree with us that the most important understanding of a concept is demonstrated by one's skill in applying it, then perhaps the reader can agree with us that the six scholars have made a fundamental mistake in the design of their empirical inquiry. They ask whether the judges understand such concepts as falsifiability, yet they are satisfied to evaluate that understanding with no more evidence than the judges' abstract statements of what the concept means; they do not try to observe how the judges apply the concept in court.

Could the six offer the response that the judges could not possibly apply the concept well if they did not at least understand its abstract meaning? We do not believe that this is a good response. Our first objection to this response is to remind the reader of the social context in which the judge operates—judges perform their tasks in a courtroom, not in a study or a laboratory. At trial, a judge would never apply the concept unaided and singly. An expert would testify that a theory being used is truly scientific because it is both falsifiable and has not yet been falsified. The judge would have the benefit of the expert's explanation of this thesis. Furthermore, the expert's explanation would be tested by cross-examination and by the testimony of other experts, who might agree, qualify, or disagree. So the relevant question is not whether a judge can understand the concept unaided, but whether the judge can respond appropriately to disputes over falsifiability when aided by what happens in court. We see no reason to assume that there would be other than a random correlation between abstract understanding prior to trial and the concrete understanding that would follow a trial.

Our second objection to the response that abstract knowledge is necessary is that even outside the courtroom, such an assumption is false. We rest our objection on the well-known distinction between "knowing how" and "knowing that." To take a trivial example, most children are able to learn *how* to ride a bicycle. But what do they know when they know how to ride a bike? The child does not know exactly what it does in a technical sense when riding the bike, nor do we, nor do the six scholars, we expect. It takes a highly trained scientific mind to gain an abstract knowledge of the facts of bike riding. Furthermore, the example is not off the point merely because it involves a physical skill. Intellectual skills have the same quality, and for them too, one can know *how* to do something without knowing *what* it is that one knows. Merely because one is a highly skilled trial lawyer does not mean that one has a conscious intellectual understanding of what it is that one knows. Indeed, we understand that one of the major research projects in cognitive psychology today is to understand what precisely it is that people know when they know how to do all of the things that they are able to do.[36]

For all of these reasons, we think that the six scholars asked the judges the wrong questions. But their fundamental error, for the purposes of this book, is that they constructed an abstract ideal of science and then used that abstraction to criticize what is done with science in the courtroom. Our fundamental disagreement is that one should not start by making this mistake. This error—isolating a methodology from the way it is used—can be seen in the work of many legal scholars.

Overemphasizing Methodology, Ignoring the Context

Characterizing science as singularly methodological can function to eclipse the social aspects of science. Professor Neil Cohen, for example, in his commentary on evidentiary gatekeeping by judges, pejoratively describes the process by which data are given to a forensic expert, who draws conclusions by an "analysis [that] takes place out of sight of the factfinders."

> An example of that model might be . . . a . . . handwriting expert, who is given samples . . . analyzes them, and pronounces the document [in question] to have been written (or not . . .) by the defendant. While the expert might recite the factors that lead . . . to the conclusion, the process by which those factors are weighed and balanced, as well as the justification for using those factors and not others, takes place in the expert's mind.[37]

By contrast, for Cohen, "the testimony of epidemiologists and scientists using similar methods . . . is based on expertise that takes place in a 'clear box' in which the entire thought process of the expert can be monitored and assessed."[38] We appreciate the emphasis on application in this quotation. We note, however, that Cohen is not really interested in revealing the pragmatic and socially contingent features of an expert's testimony. From Cohen's scientistic perspective, all we want to see (through the "clear box") is hypothesis, data, methodology, and result. In other words, science *itself* has been idealized as an almost mechanical producer of knowledge, while the expert, along with the social context that makes science possible, has disappeared.

Following his idealization of science, Cohen argues that since scientific standards are too high for law, expert opinions that would not qualify as "real" science should be allowed into court.[39] Like others who believe that plaintiffs in civil suits are treated unfairly by the restrictive *Daubert* Trilogy regime, Cohen believes that the burden of proof in science is much higher than the preponderance of evidence standard in the courtroom (Cohen presumes, wrongly we think, that "more probable than not" means "statistically greater than 50%," which presumption oversimplifies the process of analysis that ordinary people use when they decide something has been proven);[40] this leads Cohen to suggest, somewhat strangely, that scientific experts should testify as nonscientists, perhaps by stating: "I would not proclaim in an academic paper the existence of a link between the medication and high blood pressure" because I could not meet "stringent scientific standards," but in "this setting, I would set the threshold somewhat lower [and proclaim a link], which I believe more accurately reflects the balance of considerations in this setting."[41]

If science were a disembodied methodology, as Cohen believes, then his proposal would be logical. Such a methodology would be far too pure to be applied by judges and juries, so of necessity, one would have to accept adulterated science, not pure science, in the courtroom. Fortunately, Cohen is wrong, since his proposal is also highly impractical. How could a scientist testify under Cohen's regime? (I am a scientist, but I am supposed to testify to something that doesn't meet my standards of science?) And what would the jury think? (Do these scientific witnesses believe their own testimony? What are we supposed to do with a scientist who testifies to nonscience?) In short, we believe that Cohen's proposal is a vivid example of the danger of idealizing science generally, and of the particular danger of idealizing scientific methodology.

Overemphasizing Junk Science

Because scientific methodology is not a uniform, mechanical producer of knowledge, and because scientists who share a commitment to methodological conventions often disagree, we wish to suggest that casual use of the phrase "junk science" is unfortunate. James Shellow, for example, in his commentary on the limits of cross-examination of experts, begins by identifying "junk scientists" who were supposed to be exposed in "*Daubert* and *Kumho* hearings," who "[u]nfortunately appear on the stand well-dressed and articulate," and who "believe in their junk science." Shellow subsequently refers to "now legendary junk science,"[42] but his term "legendary" is more appropriate than he might realize. Professor John Mansfield has appropriately condemned the "campaign of sloganeering, employing such labels as 'junk science' . . . aimed at casting scorn on those who testified to opinions thought to warrant these labels. It is embarrassing to concede that this kind of sloganeering may have influenced the course of the law."[43] We acknowledge that not all proffered expertise is adequate: some experts and some expertise are not worthy of the courtroom. Even so, the "model that posits junk science as distinguishable from . . . 'good science' . . . is a flexible, politically charged framework that . . . plays a strategic, rhetorical role in the agendas of many who attempt to address the pervasive perception of an ongoing legal crisis."[44] Not everyone who talks about junk science is a knave, but the term is loose and dangerous.

As Professors Gary Edmond and David Mercer argue, the junk science model relies on "untenable images of efficacy, methods, norms, and motivations as hallmarks of 'good science.'"[45] The term *junk science*, lacking any consistent meaning, functions more as an ideal or image for those who

(i) oversimplify the relationship between scientific knowledge and technically efficacious outcomes

(ii) view "factors like financial opportunism [as] hallmarks of junk science, [when] in reality such factors provide powerful motors for many fields of contemporary science"

(iii) consider scientific norms prescribing that scientists be detached, impersonal, self-critical, and open-minded as "necessary feature[s] of doing scientific work"

(iv) assume that "a simple, identifiable, universal scientific method . . . guides [scientific] activity[46]

In short, the very mention of junk science, unless it is qualified immediately with carefully examined examples, signals a romanticization of science as method and a corresponding failure to acknowledge the social context *of even the best science* as constitutive.

Modest Views of Science: Acknowledging the Context

Although the tendency to overidealize science is widespread among legal scholars, we are happy to report that many do recognize that the social context of science can help generate good science. Professor Margaret Berger, for example, describes DNA typing as "the by-product of cutting-edge science," as opposed to "forensic specialties which originated within the law enforcement community . . . to facilitate investigations and prosecutions."[47] The distinction between cutting-edge science and "courtroom" science might appear to support an argument that the latter is social—motivated, biased (toward prosecution), and interested—as opposed to the former as relatively objective or natural. In her historical narrative concerning DNA typing, however, Berger speaks of that method's universal ratification by the scientific community, of scientists serving on committees to monitor the use of DNA typing in trials, of reports issued by the National Academy of Sciences, of shifts in laboratory technologies, of impliedly valid disputes concerning "appropriate probabilities and . . . how they should be expressed," of the need for proper collection and analysis of genetic markers, of quality control and documentation protocols in laboratories, and of "proficiency testing of laboratory personnel."[48] Two observations about this list can be made. First, each of the listed phenomena is decidedly social, institutional, or rhetorical (not simply methodological): community ratification, committees, institutional reports, evolving technologies and protocols, disputes, document writing, and credentialing. Second, these social features of DNA typing have generated good not bad science; without the elaborate social process that Berger documents, DNA typing would not have made the progress that it has. Note, however, that Berger does not idealize nuclear DNA testing—"the gold standard for expert proof"—because it "may, under some circumstances, produce results that are completely wrong." Reliability in the abstract, therefore, is not enough. For admissibility and sufficiency determinations, the focus should be on "what the evidence proves and how the trier of fact will use it."[49]

In his critique of experts who peddle "tainted or fraudulent science," Professor Paul Giannelli offers a similar description of good science.[50] Giannelli summarizes the recommendations of the Inspector General's 1997 report on the FBI laboratory. The report criticized inaccurate, incompetent, and poorly documented testimony, and recommended

> (1) seeking accreditation of the FBI laboratory by the American Society of Crime Laboratory Directors/Laboratory Accreditation Board; (2) requiring examiners . . . to have scientific backgrounds . . . ; (3) mandating the preparation . . . of separate reports instead of having one composite report . . . ; (4) establishing report review procedures . . . ; (5) preparing adequate case files . . . ; (6) monitoring court testimony . . . ; and (7) developing written protocols for scientific procedures.[51]

The keys to legitimate scientific inquiry are the social, not just methodological, aspects of science (institutional accreditation, credentialing, review of documentation, and procedural conventions). Institutions, community oversight, persuasive documentation, and the social capital represented by credentials are the cure for mediocre science and the route to scientific progress. In light of these accounts, the counterargument that the social, institutional, and rhetorical aspects of science are secondary to science's *real* or methodological work (hypothesis, data, and testing), rings hollow.

Finally, we should mention Professor Christopher Slobogin's recent commentary on expertise in criminal cases, which concedes the difficulties faced by defendants using social scientists in the exclusionary post-*Daubert* regime (for example, error rates are hard to generate because of multiple variables and the practical and ethical limitations on experimentation).[52] Slobogin notes that research "requires money [and] the state has more of it."

> The state not only has more money, but it is better equipped, in an institutional sense, to use it . . . . [T]he state is better able to anticipate the scientific issues that will arise and act accordingly. Indeed, *Daubert* and *Kumho Tire* have already stimulated massive federal efforts to validate the type of forensic evidence typically relied upon by the prosecution.[53]

The resources of defense-oriented academic researchers "pale when compared to the government's."[54] In this context, Slobogin is not *criticizing* prosecution-oriented science for its interest, bias, or motivation; rather, Slobogin contends that methodology *needs* institutional support. Money and other resources are, almost always, conditions for the production of scientific expertise.[55]

Any discussion of institutional support must lead inevitably to a focus on the political aspect of science and its relevance to those who study the process of making policy in agencies and legislatures. We regularly read complaints that science is ignored because of political pressures, which is no doubt true. However, science is not pure, and sometimes political values are relevant. One should always use the best science available and in the best way, whether one is a legislature, an agency, or a court. However, we should not imagine that science is a magic wand that with one wave can solve all social problems; to do so is to idealize.

MODEST VERSUS IDEALIZED VIEWS OF LAW

In the Seton Hall Symposium, some solutions to the perceived challenges (for lawyers and judges) generated by the *Daubert* Trilogy often took the form of idealizing a particular element of the trial: perhaps the process of appellate review, the jury, the trial judge, or even lawyers. Like idealizations of science, idealizations of law tend to deflect attention away from the application phase. In the "case at hand," notions of reliability and validity intersect with confidence levels and the pragmatic goals and limitations of scientific inquiry. Moreover, just as idealizations of science are bolstered by downplaying or demonizing (as unscientific) the social aspects of science, idealizations of particular features of law often rely on demonizations of other aspects: appellate panels correct the unruly discretion of trial judges; trial judges correct the deficiencies of juries; juries correct adversarial excess or exaggerated expertise; and good lawyers police bad experts. Failure to recognize the realistic limits of law, as well as science, will result in impractical reform proposals.

Idealizing Appellate Courts

Recall that on appeal, appellate courts review a trial judge's admissibility decisions on the basis of the abuse-of-discretion standard—if the trial judge was "in the ball park" and not obviously in error in the exercise of his or her discretion, an admissibility decision will not be reversed. Some scholars, however, criticize that standard and argue for plenary or de novo review of a judge's evaluation of an expert, in which an appellate panel would decide for itself whether the trial judge got it right. We view the latter argument as an idealization of appellate judges as the solution to the problem of bad science in the courtroom. For example, Professor Christopher Mueller suggests that appellate review of admissibility decisions (concerning expertise) should be de novo.[56] Mueller is convinced that the abuse-of-discretion standard, confirmed in *Joiner* and *Kumho Tire*, will lead to an unfortunate lack of uniformity.

> [I]ssues relating to the validity of theories and techniques transcend the facts of individual cases. This observation applies . . . to the question whether DNA profiling can reliably identify a blood or fluid sample as having very likely come from one person . . . . It applies to the question whether proffered statistical proof should satisfy the standard that scientists would require, to . . . whether differential diagnosis . . . [,] animal studies . . . , and . . . similarities between . . . chemical structures . . . can prove causation. Questions of this magnitude need steadier guidance than the abuse-of-discretion standard provides, and the answers that courts reach should be applied in similar cases . . . .[57]

In our view, the term *abuse-of-discretion* is indeed notorious for its elasticity of meaning; appellate courts regularly reverse trial judges and administrative agencies under this heading. Lack of uniformity, however, in deciding cases is not an evil unless the cases are indistinguishable. If the appropriate question in cases involving scientific expertise is primarily how science is brought to bear in a particular case, and not scientific reliability in general, then the reliability ruling in any particular case is likely to be easily distinguishable from other rulings. Furthermore, first-rate science could be correctly applied in one case, but bungled in another; if so, uniformity is not desirable. To be sure, the current regime does not generate certainty, but we believe that the desire for certainty springs from a false idealization, of law, of science, or of both.

Idealizing the Jury

In addition to idealizations of appellate review (to correct deficient judges), some scholars at the Seton Hall Symposium idealized the jury. Professor John Mansfield, for example, argues that the rules of evidence have been, are, and should be oriented to the admission of all relevant evidence. Thus, *Daubert*'s reliability requirement for admissibility ends up as an embarrassing error. Moreover, given that the reliability requirement leads judges to invade the province of the jury, Mansfield believes this error has constitutional dimensions.[58]

To bolster his idealization of the jury, Mansfield demonizes those who hope *Daubert*'s reliability requirements will improve the accuracy of adjudication. As Mansfield sees it, *Daubert* was the product of "powerful economic interests," "the desire of some judges to be associated with science," "the anger and scorn [of] elite scientists" toward law, and "an ideology, far from decisively eliminated in our political debates, which cannot see the sense in entrusting to twelve persons picked at random from the general population important and difficult questions of fact."[59] Singled out as an ideologue, Professor Ronald Allen is allegedly guilty of the fourth count in Mansfield's indictment. Allen's emphasis on accuracy in trials is said to rest on the "conviction that jury verdicts are not as accurate as other forms of adjudication and that there is no good policy reason why an inferior form of fact-finding should be accepted."[60] We shall ignore the first three counts in Mansfield's indictment and focus on the fourth.

Though Mansfield suggests that *Kumho Tire* is incompatible with respect for the jury, one can admire both *Kumho Tire* and the jury system: judge plus jury is superior to judge or jury alone. The rules of evidence, enforced by a judge, can lead to presenting better evidence to a jury than otherwise would be presented. Better evidence is more likely to lead to better decisions. The difficulty lies in formulating the best working relationship between counsel, judge, and jury, and we shall spare the reader from a tedious discourse on procedure. We shall simply make three bold and undocumented statements and then pass on: (i) only a madman could claim that the present system is efficient, but efficiency without justice is repellant; (ii) combining legal expertise (the judge) with the common sense of the community (the jury) is the best hope of our culture for justice; (iii) constructing the best architecture for this system of shared power between judge and jury is a never-ending task.

Idealizing the Trial Judge

Professor David Faigman is the best representative of those who idealize the trial judge's role. Responding to those scholars who tend to idealize the jury and seek "to retain a prominent role for jurors in the evaluation of scientific evidence," Faigman is dismissive:

> The issue of judge versus jury . . . is largely irrelevant. It is the judge's task to evaluate the validity of proffered expert testimony, and that is all there is to it. . . . The only question is what is the nature of the judge's job in this regard—the rest will be done by the jury.[61]

According to Faigman, moreover, trial judges should attend not simply to what happens to expertise in court, but also "to what occurred before the expertise reached the courtroom and . . . what might happen to the expertise subsequently." While we agree that an "admissibility decision necessarily requires a policy judgment" insofar as the scientific community does not provide answers to legal questions, Faigman goes further and states that "the evidentiary determination regarding expert evidence must . . . integrate into its foundational premises . . . the culture of the scientific method."[62] Since we reject any notion of "legal" science disengaged from actual scientific practices, even that sounds agreeable, so long as one does not romanticize the possibilities. But for Faigman's trial judge, it is a two-way street. Judges should not only "ask whether better evidence is available, [but] whether better evidence should be available . . . . [If handwriting experts lack data, the] issue is whether the courts should expect the scientific community (broadly defined) to have produced better data on handwriting."[63] Faigman's trial judges, therefore, have the responsibility of considering the "ramifications of their admissibility decisions both in regard to the development of the respective expertise and in terms of the costs of errors . . . for society at-large." Anticipating criticism of this tall order, Faigman concedes that "many will complain about the difficulty of the task. It is true that [this] complicates the judge's job. But so be it. Science is complicated."[64]

One would be hard pressed to imagine a more fantastic proposal than Faigman's, under which trial judges must consider the probable consequences of their decisions on (i) creating incentives or disincentives for scientific research, and (ii) reducing or increasing error rates by adjudicating. Imagine the plight of a trial judge who must decide whether the lawyers are presenting reliable evidence on whether drug *x* caused disease *y*. Faigman would add to the agenda; the trial judge should also ask, "Will this decision become known among those who allocate resources for research in a way that increases or decreases incentives?" and "Will this decision be accepted as a precedent by other judges in a way that increases or decreases the error rates in future trials?" We confidently predict that the judiciary will not embrace this role. Most judges do not lack self-esteem, but few are immodest, as is Faigman's ideal judge.

Idealizing Lawyers

A lawyer's reasonable belief that evidence is false does not preclude its presentation to the trier of fact.[65]

Assume that you are litigating a case involving issues for which scientific testimony is relevant. Assume further that generally accepted scientific consensus is in your adversary's favor, so that any science you will present is less than compelling. Nevertheless, you and your client are able to find an expert who will testify in your favor. If you genuinely doubt the accuracy of that expert's testimony, do you have any responsibility, under the rules of professional conduct or due to higher goals of professionalism, to alter your trial strategy (e.g., refuse to use the doubtful scientific testimony), or can you proceed zealously to build your case on the basis of your questionable expert's scientific opinion?

That inquiry has all the markings of a classical ethical dilemma in law. Not only are the applicable rules of professional conduct somewhat ambiguous, but there is the characteristic conflict between fidelity to one's client and duties to the court. Moreover, a tension persists between what the rules allow and what a higher sense of professionalism might not. Finally, this is an area where the avowedly ethical practice of advocates—proffering shaky or doubtful scientific expertise on behalf of a client—confirms the public's fear that attorneys regularly *buy* expertise in a market where somebody will testify to just about anything.[66] (We will now plunge into a legal discourse on professional ethics, and we acknowledge that a non-lawyer may be reluctant to read straight through. As an incentive, we assert that the next several pages will give our non-lawyer readers a chance to decide for themselves whether that which lawyers call legal ethics is a comedy, a tragedy, or some third thing.)

Long before the recent Enron debacle and the resulting call for a higher sense of responsibility for corporate fraud on the part of outside corporate counsel,[67] the perception of (and debate concerning) junk science in the courtroom raised the question whether attorneys were to blame.[68] Two relatively extreme positions on that question are nowadays identifiable: (i) attorneys neither vouch for their experts' opinions nor serve as gatekeepers with respect to the admissibility or validity of courtroom science,[69] and (ii) it is about time for lawyers to take more responsibility for junk science—the latter of which discredits our legal system and leads to outrageous and inconsistent verdicts.[70] Both positions oversimplify the role of attorneys as advocates, the former by ignoring obvious circumstances where responsibility arises, and the latter by its tendency to see scientific knowledge as unproblematic. As we will show, some of the appeals for more responsibility (with respect to experts) on the part of lawyers are linked to an idealized view of science.

The Ethics of Presenting Expert Testimony

> As an advocate in the adversary system, it is a lawyer's job to make the best possible argument in support of her client. A lawyer will often find herself advancing a position in the hope that it will work, without necessarily believing that the view is correct.[71]

Such indirect language is the norm in the literature on the ethics of presenting scientific testimony.[72] Even Rule 3.3(a)(3), which clearly *allows* an attorney to offer evidence reasonably believed to be false, actually says that a "lawyer may *refuse* to offer evidence . . . that the lawyer reasonably believes is false."[73] In the 2002 version of the *ABA Model Rules*, the earlier (1983) comment that "an advocate does not vouch for the evidence submitted" was sanitized by placing "although" before the clause and adding (after the clause) a duty to ensure that the tribunal is not misled by "evidence that the lawyer knows to be false." It is as if we lawyers are in denial, or ashamed, of our discretion to offer evidence we believe to be false.

Viewing Rule 3.3(a)(3) as an exhaustive set of categories in which to place expert testimony, there are three possibilities: (i) evidence that is known to be false *cannot* be offered, (ii) evidence that is known *or* believed to be true *can* (obviously) be offered, and (iii) evidence that is *believed* to be false can also be offered.[74] With respect to scientific expertise, the situations in which an attorney *knows* that an expert is wrong would seem to be quite rare. In Virginia, for example, *knowledge* of fraudulent testimony is established by acknowledgment of the fraud by the expert, which of course leaves little doubt on the part of the attorney.[75] Short of such an acknowledgment, however, attorneys may often have serious doubts about an expert but no knowledge of falsity, which seems to relieve attorneys from responsibility for shaky or less-than-credible science.

On the other hand, the rules may not be as generous as they first appear. First, Comment 8 to Rule 3.3, and Rule 1.0 (f) which is cited in that comment, confirms that knowledge of falsity "can be inferred from the circumstances," and also that a "lawyer cannot ignore an obvious falsehood."[76] This comment raises the possibility that a lawyer claiming not to know of an expert's falsehoods may be disbelieved and may be deemed to have actual knowledge of them because they are so obvious to others. Just as one can be convicted on the basis of circumstantial evidence, a lawyer's claim not to know can be second-guessed. Moreover, some commentators highlight the term *reasonable* in Rule 3.3 and its official commentary—"A lawyer's reasonable belief that evidence is false does not preclude its presentation. . . ."[77]—and suggest that the lawyer's uncertainty must be "genuine *and* reasonable."[78] That is, if one's belief that a certain expert's testimony is false is so strong that one really has no "genuine and reasonable" doubt that it is false, and one is only categorizing it as a belief for strategic reasons, the belief may be transformed into knowledge of falsity. Finally, there is the suggestion in some judicial opinions (discussed below) that knowledge of falsity can be imputed if the lawyer *should have known* of that falsity, which raises the specter of a duty to inquire or even to confirm suspicions.

In *Harre v. A.H. Robins Co., Inc.*, a Dalkon Shield case, a doctor serving as an expert for the defendant testified at trial that he had directed certain tests, implying that he had personally conducted the experiments.[79] Shortly thereafter in another case, the same expert was questioned by the same attorney, and this time testified that he had neither conducted nor supervised such tests.[80] On appeal of the trial verdict in the earlier case, the court concluded that the expert had testified falsely *and* that defense counsel "knew *or should have known* of the falsity of the testimony."[81]

> [In] view of the fact that Dr. Keith had acted as a consultant/expert for Robins attorneys since 1977, it becomes obvious that Robins' counsel must have been aware [of the contradictory testimony] . . . .
>
> This court is deeply disturbed by the fact that a material expert witness, with complicity of counsel, would falsely testify on the ultimate issue of causation.[82]

In other words, as soon as an expert's testimony is contradictory, the usual discretion to offer evidence believed to be false—based on the notion that the lawyer does not vouch for an expert's testimony if the lawyer does not *know* it is false—is lost. The falsehood is *obvious*, and if the lawyer claims merely to have doubts about the testimony but not knowledge of its falsity, those doubts are not *genuine and reasonable*.

Another recent case with similar facts, *McNeil v. the Atchison, Topeka and Santa Fe Railway Company*, involved an employee who won a verdict (based on expert testimony by the employee's treating physicians) for a permanent disability.[83] Eight days later, the employee tried to return to his former position, and when his former employer refused, the employee filed a discrimination suit claiming he had been rehabilitated. The court, "astonished by the audacity of the Plaintiff," remarked that

> absent a representation of outright Divine Intervention, . . . the Court is left with an uncomfortable inference of outright fraud . . . .
>
> * * *
>
> Given the egregious conduct of Plaintiff and the apparent willing complicity of his counsel, this Court is not at all surprised by the current public outcry for tort reform . . . .[84]

Here, instead of offering contradictory or new testimony alerting counsel to falsity, the second claim was inconsistent with the expert testimony in the first. The circumstances suggested an obvious falsehood, arguably leaving the attorney without any genuine and reasonable doubt as to the falsity of his client's claim.

These cases together suggest expansions of the category of *known* falsities that cannot be offered, as well as corresponding contractions of the category of evidence "reasonably believed to be false" that can be offered. Actual knowledge can be inferred from circumstances, and even constructive knowledge (e.g., *Harre*'s "known or should have known" phrase) of an obvious falsehood places limits on claims of "genuine and reasonable doubt but not knowledge." Whether an attorney has an additional duty of due diligence and reasonable inquiry to confirm doubts about an expert's testimony is not clear, but some scholars have suggested that when a lawyer reasonably believes, but does not know, that an expert will testify falsely, that genuine and reasonable doubt could be treated as knowledge of falsity if, "in the exercise of due diligence upon reasonable inquiry,"[85] the attorney *should know* the testimony to be false.

That position has been suggested by one commentator on Rule 3.4—which prohibits falsifying evidence—who asserted that Rule 3.4 "forbids an attorney to permit an expert to testify as an expert in an area that is not scientifically valid."[86] Such an interpretation idealistically implies that an attorney should or could determine the scientific validity of an expert's opinion. Significantly, this interpretation is not qualified by the attorney's knowledge of scientific validity, as in Rule 3.3, but rather sets up scientific validity as a standard for what we *know* or *should know* to be true or false. This, we think, is an extreme view that is not warranted by the rules of professional conduct. Even as we identify bases for more responsibility on the part of attorneys with respect to their experts, we think that there is a risk of idealizing science as an unproblematic standard for truth. Even scientists disagree about the validity of many hypotheses, thus it hardly makes sense to require that lawyers make evaluations of scientific validity, or even to assume that lawyers know when a hypothesis is true.

Junk Science: Who's to Blame?

> When all else fails—when neither improved pretrial procedures nor strengthened ethical codes succeed in terminating litigation in which one party's position is grounded solely on specious expert testimony—it may be the task of the judge to do what the adversarial process and professional ethics have failed to do.[87]

That statement by Chief Judge Jack Weinstein in 1986 impliedly recognized the safe haven (in the rules of professional conduct) that allows lawyers to present expert testimony that is reasonably believed to be false. Indeed, Judge Weinstein's article was full of suggestions to eliminate frivolous and obfuscating expert testimony—including revised procedural rules and rules of evidence, control of experts by outside agencies, substantive law reform, use of neutral experts, stronger controls by courts, and scientific enlightenment of judges—but lawyers were not the direct target of his critique. Arguably in response to concerns over junk science in the courtroom, the U.S. Supreme

Court in *Daubert* reinforced the gatekeeping role of judges and offered a legal standard for scientific validity. Shortly thereafter, the Federal Rules of Evidence were amended to confirm that admissible scientific testimony must be "based upon sufficient facts or data" and be "the product of reliable principles and methods" that have been applied "reliably to the facts of the case."[88] Viewed as a cure for junk science, the new federal jurisprudence of law and science relations placed the responsibility on trial judges and evidentiary rules, not on lawyers. Lawyers are advocates, and when you read an appellate opinion reversing a trial judge's admissibility determination, the trial judge may well be admonished for failing to be a gatekeeper;[89] but lawyers are rarely blamed for trying to introduce doubtful scientific testimony.

Some scholars, however, do claim that lawyers have an ethical obligation to keep junk science out of the courtroom. For example, Dick Thornburgh, former U.S. attorney general, boldly asserts that "it is unethical lawyers who are largely to blame for junk science."[90]

> It is clear that the lawyer does have a duty to determine whether he believes expert testimony will be admissible before trying to introduce such evidence in court . . . . To be an effective advocate, the lawyer must . . . test the accuracy and reliability of . . . expert testimony . . . he wishes to introduce.[91]

Thornburgh bases this argument on the duty in Rule 3.1 to bring only meritorious (i.e., not frivolous) claims and contentions,[92] which he interprets as requiring that, prior to introducing an expert, lawyers ensure "that there is a good faith basis to believe that [the proffered testimony] is reliable scientific evidence."[93] Thornburgh even suggests that Rule 11 sanctions would be appropriate if "it is discovered before the conclusion of the proceedings that certain evidence presented was, in fact, junk science."[94]

It is simply not clear whether Thornburgh is arguing for law reform or is claiming that the current rules of professional conduct already make lawyers ethically responsible for policing junk science. He concedes that "an attorney's ethical obligations would not be enough to prevent the admission of junk science," since lawyers are allowed to proffer expert testimony they reasonably believe is false, but then he refers to "the full recognition of the lawyer's professional obligation to carefully scrutinize the integrity of his own expert's proposed testimony . . . ."[95] To the extent that Thornburgh bases this latter ethical obligation on the lawyer's duty to bring only meritorious claims and contentions, we see at least three problems with his analysis. First, after he claims the "ethical rules . . . require that a lawyer must insure there is a good faith basis for the admissibility of evidence," he concedes that lawyers "have no clear guidelines on what will, or will not, be deemed admissible scientific expert testimony."[96] Second, any ethical obligation to ensure *reliable* testimony would be inconsistent with the lawyer's discretion to present expert testimony reasonably believed (but not *known*) to be false.

This brings us to our third, and most important, concern: Thornburgh's frustrated attempt to find some basis for the ethical responsibility of lawyers regarding junk science is coupled with an idealized view of science. His preferred solution for the problem of junk science, a "court-appointed board of experts or advisory panel,"[97] signifies his confidence in science itself as neutral and disinterested. Indeed, the examples of cases and controversies that Thornburgh offers to conceptualize his discussion of the ethical responsibilities of lawyers[98] are presented as involving two opposing kinds of evidence: genuine science and junk science. That tendency to see good science versus junk science in law, rather than scientific *theories* in *conflict*, is indicative of a particular view of science as a field that is far removed and different from law. Law is, in this view, unstable, adversarial, rhetorical, institutional, and value-laden, while science is characterized by universal standards, rigorous methodologies and testing, and consensus. Given that picture, it is not surprising that commentators like Thornburgh both (i) recommend neutral science panels to stabilize legal disputes, and (ii) criticize attorneys for their ethical shortcomings. Why don't attorneys just, in Thornburgh's words, "test the reliability and accuracy of" their experts' testimony and reject experts who lack "integrity"?[99] The very question presumes that in any scientific dispute in court, it will be obvious that one expert is wrong and the other is right, and that a lawyer who presents the first expert is unethical and knows it.

Any analysis of the ethical responsibility of lawyers to evaluate their experts' testimony must take into account the complexities and uncertainty of scientific knowledge. While some lawyers are trained scientists, most would not consider themselves to be, in Thornburgh's account, "a gatekeeper of sorts . . . to prevent junk science from pervading our courtrooms."[100] In some circumstances, when a lawyer knows that an expert is testifying falsely, the rules of professional conduct prohibit the lawyer from offering that testimony; but otherwise, the reasonable belief (on a lawyer's part) of truth or falsity is not given much weight in trial proceedings. The suggestion that a lawyer who has doubts about an expert's testimony should treat these doubts as an identification of junk science is based on a view of scientific controversies as relatively straightforward—that is, as good science versus junk science. If, on the other hand, scientific controversies often involve two competing views, each with its own methodological preferences, theoretical biases, and institutional affiliations, then the lawyer's ethical role is to ensure that the client's best evidence gets a hearing.

Idealizing Lawyers and Science

[J]udges confronted with expert conflict need to resist the extreme labels of both "pure science" and "junk science," neither of which well characterizes the scientific foundations of evidence, while remaining open to all available knowledge that meets threshold tests of relevance and reliability . . . . They must strive to develop a sixth sense . . . for ways in which bias can creep into even well-intentioned forms of scientific inquiry, as well as for the differences between legitimately divergent viewpoints and truly marginal claims of expertise.[101]

Lawyers dealing with expert scientific witnesses likewise need to develop that sixth sense, while resisting extreme labels like "junk science," keeping relevance and reliability in mind as the legal standards, and recognizing that a legitimate scientific controversy does not necessitate portraying one side as inept. There are, of course, compelling arguments for the position that attorneys should be more responsible for bad experts. If an expert, even one who does not admit to lying, testifies inconsistently, the lawyer can no longer take advantage of the reasonable-doubt-but-no-knowledge safe haven. Similarly, if a lawyer has reasonable doubts that could easily be confirmed, the lawyer should not be allowed to remain in blissful ignorance. On the other hand, scientific knowledge, which arises in a field that in recent decades has been known for its dynamic change, is not easily confirmed or refuted. Those who argue that attorneys are capable of fulfilling an ethical responsibility to keep junk science out of the courtroom are often not only arguing for a change in the traditional role of advocacy, which in limited circumstances is compelling, but also asking that we idealize lawyers and science.

As our review of post-*Daubert* discourse demonstrates, the idealizations of particular aspects of law—of appellate panels, of juries, of trial judges, and of lawyers—have resulted in impractical proposals. Sometimes, as with Professor John Mansfield, idealization of the jury interferes with our ability to appreciate *Kumho Tire*'s emphasis on the "case at hand." For Mansfield, *any* reliability standard, even one that realistically acknowledges the pragmatic character of the scientific enterprise and the diversity of its methodologies, poses a threat to the jury's role.[102] With respect to the other scholars discussed here, idealization of appellate review, the trial judge, or ethical lawyers also deflects attention away from the application phase, because the difficult problem of evaluating science is evaded by imagining an arbiter above the fray. In our view, the application phase includes fallible but typically competent lawyers, experts, trial judges, juries, and appellate judges, each of whom has a corrective role to play. Neither demonizing nor idealizing any one of them is necessary (or helpful), and avoiding such tendencies keeps the focus on the production of evidence for the "case at hand."

Recognizing the practical limitations of both science and law helps scholars to avoid impractical proposals for reform. Romantic images of appellate courts fail to recognize their limited resources. Romantic images of trial judges over-estimate their capacity to criticize expertise and make "science policy" decisions. Romantic images of ethical lawyers ignore the role of an advocate. And romantic images of the jury disengage science from law. Moreover, proposals to raise the admissibility standards for forensic scientists, or to lower them for civil trial plaintiffs, if successful, could engender other changes to the legal system. To illustrate, if courts agree to go easier on plaintiffs' experts, tort-reform advocates might gain the upper hand. And in the criminal law context, we endorse Professor R. Erik Lillquist's humorous and shrewd suggestion that if

> Judge Pollak had stuck to his decision in *United States v. Llera Plaza*, limiting the testimony of the government's fingerprint examiners and forbidding them from opining that a particular print is from a particular person . . . it seems to me at least possible, if not likely, that Congress would have quickly passed legislation entitled something like the Latent Fingerprint Admissibility Act of 2002.[103]

We agree that changes in one area of the law can generate a backlash. Therefore, solutions must take into account the practical context. In the area of admissibility of scientific expertise, for example, arguments for restrictiveness that rest on idealizations of science are met with arguments that idealize the jury to overcome those restrictions. So long as one modestly views both science and law as pragmatic enterprises, *Daubert*'s focus on application can work in its present form without raising or lowering reliability standards, and without changing the abuse-of-discretion standard or the current role of judges as gatekeepers, lawyers as advocates, and jurors as beneficiaries of a gatekeeping regime.

Having discussed the idealization of science among judges and legal scholars, and having set forth the contours of a modest view of science, we turn in the next chapter to some novel evidence that science is a pragmatic activity, which can be demonstrated by listening to the narratives of scientists themselves in pretrial depositions and in ethnographic interviews. But before we leave this chapter, we wish to make another comment about the analogy between courts and administrative agencies. When Justice Stephen Breyer was Judge Stephen Breyer, he proposed creating an elite corps of scientific bureaucrats who could move about from agency to agency.[104] While this proposal might have merit, we doubt that it would solve the problem of using science in policy as Breyer thought it might. We think that Breyer has unduly idealized what bureaucrats can do, just as David Faigman idealized what judges can do.

NOTES

1. John M. Barry, *Rising Tide: The Great Mississippi Flood of 1927 and How it Changed America* 42 (1997) (quoting comments of Andrew Atkinson Humphreys).

2. "Expert Admissibility Symposium: Reliability Standards—Too High, Too Low, or Just Right?" 33 *Seton Hall L. Rev.* 881 (2003); "Expert Admissibility Symposium: What Is the Question? What Is the Answer? How Should the Court Frame a Question to Which Standards of Reliability Are to be Applied?" 34 *Seton Hall L. Rev.* 1 (2003) (proceedings of February 21–22, 2003, Symposium).

3. 522 U.S. 136 (1997); 526 U.S. 137 (1999).

4. Ronald J. Allen, "Expertise and the Supreme Court: What Is the Problem?" 34 *Seton Hall L. Rev.* 1, 7 (2003).

5. Samuel R. Gross and Jennifer L. Mnookin, "Expert Information and Expert Evidence: A Preliminary Taxonomy," 34 *Seton Hall L. Rev.* 141, 143 (2003).

6. *Id.* at 143–44.

7. Michael J. Saks, "The Legal and Scientific Evaluation of Forensic Science (Especially Fingerprint Expert Testimony)," 33 *Seton Hall L. Rev.* 1167, 1169 (2003). To illustrate, the peer review and publication factor is not determinative of admissibility because, as Professor Moreno points out, that factor in the abstract "tells us nothing about . . . whether the validity of the published methods or conclusions is [relevant to] the manner in which this expert proposes to *use* the theory or technique to make inferences or draw conclusions in the case." *See* Joëlle Anne Moreno, "Eyes Wide Shut: Hidden Problems and Future Consequences of the Fact-Based Validity Standard," 34 *Seton Hall L. Rev.* 89, 99 (2003).

8. Richard D. Friedman, Squeezing *Daubert* Out of the Picture," 33 *Seton Hall L. Rev.* 1047, 1048 (2003).

9. *Id.* at 1063. *See also* Roger C. Park, "*Daubert* on a Tilted Playing Field," 33 *Seton Hall L. Rev.* 1113, 1114 (2003) ("I share Professor Friedman's hope that better testimony about the limits of forensic science testimony, accompanied by thoughtful instructions, will lead to better results").

10. Dale A. Nance, "Reliability and the Admissibility of Experts," 34 *Seton Hall L. Rev.* 191, 242–43 (2003).

11. Saks, *supra* note 7, at 1176.

12. Friedman, *supra* note 8, at 1064.

13. 631 N.W.2d 862, 876 (Neb. 2001).

14. *See* Joseph Sanders, "The Merits of Paternalistic Justification for Restrictions on Admissibility of Expert Evidence," 33 *Seton Hall L. Rev.* 881, 938 n.246 (2003).

15. *See* Susan Haack, "Disentangling *Daubert*: An Epistemeological Study in Theory and Practice," 5 *J. Phil Sci. and L.* 1, 4(2005) [online at www.psljournal.com/archives/all/haackpaper.cfm]:

> Every kind of empirical inquiry, from the simplest everyday puzzling over the causes of delayed buses or spoiled food to the most complex investigations of detectives, of historians, of legal and literary scholars, and of scientists, involves making an informed guess

about the explanation of some event or phenomenon, figuring out the consequences of it being true, and checking how well those consequences stand up to evidence. This is the procedure of all scientists; but it is not the procedure *only* of scientists.

16. *See* John H. Mansfield, "An Embarrassing Episode in the History of Evidence of the Law of Evidence," 34 *Seton Hall L. Rev.* 77, 81 (2003) ("The truth is that . . . there is no clear understanding and agreement about what is meant by 'science,' 'good science,' or 'the scientific method'").

17. In *Daubert* on remand, plaintiff's experts were all deemed to be "experts in their respective fields"; and the "animal studies, chemical structure analyses and epidemiological data" on which they relied were not in question. One expert, however, failed to show how his conclusion that Bendectin causes limb defects was reached. The others could not show causation, but merely a possibility, *in this case. See Daubert v. Merrell Dow Pharm., Inc.*, 43 F.3d 1311, 1317–22 (9th Cir. 1995). Likewise in *Joiner*, the animal studies and the four epidemiological studies that the plaintiff's experts relied on were not in question, though a gap existed between that data and the expert opinion on causation. *See* 522 U.S. at 144–46. Finally, in *Kumho Tire*, the issue was "not the reasonableness *in general* of a tire expert's use of a visual and tactile inspection . . . . Rather, it was the reasonableness of using that approach . . . to draw a conclusion regarding *the particular matter to which the expert testimony was directly relevant*" 526 U.S. at 153–54.

18. Gary Edmond and David Mercer, "Trashing 'Junk Science,'" 1998 *Stan. Tech. L. Rev.* 3, para. 44.

19. *See* Michael F. Baumeister and Dorothea M. Capone, "Admissibility Standards as Politics: The Imperial Gate Closers Arrive!" 33 *Seton Hall L. Rev.* 1025, 1032 (2003) (stating that epidemiological and toxicological studies are probabilistic), *id.* at 1033 ("[E]pidemiological and toxicological studies are inherently incapable of establishing causation to a certainty . . . .").

20. *Id.* at 1046.

21. *Id.* at 1045.

22. *See id.* n.134 (citing Brendan McWilliams, "Copernicus and the Center of the Universe," in *Irish Times*, Feb. 19, 2003), *id.* n.136 (citing http://www.gap.dcs.st-and .ac.uk/whistory/Mathematicians/Copernicus.html); *id.* at 1046 n.141 (citing http:// www.bluete.com/literature/Biographies/Science/Copernicus.htm).

23. *See* Edmond and Mercer, *supra* note 18, at and 63:

> [T]he history of science reveals that it is common for scientists to have strong commitments to their views during the early phases of new research. Evaluated in the context of their own time and [place], the theories of . . . Copernicus relied upon leaps of faith and observations at the threshold of theoretical plausibility, together with the deliberate omission of counter arguments.

See also Stephen F. Mason, *A History of the Sciences* 127–34 (1962) (discussing Copernicus's reliance on conventional methodology; religious, purposive, and teleological arguments; medieval as well as modern explanations; and promotion of new values). With respect to Copernicus's rhetorical strategies and his interaction with other scientists, *see generally* Jean Dietz Moss, *Novelties in the Heavens: Rhetoric and Science in the Copernican Controversy* (1993).

24. Sophia Gatowski, Shirley Dobbin, James Richardson, Gerald Ginsburg, Mara Merlino, and Veronica Dahir, "Asking the Gatekeepers: A National Survey of Judges on Judging Expert Evidence in a Post-*Daubert* World," 25 *L. and Hum. Beh.* 433, 433 (2001) (surveying four hundred state trial court judges).

25. *Id.* at 443.

26. *See id.* at 444–47, 455.

27. *See id.* at 437 ("the Court provided little if any guidance as to the meaning or application of the [*Daubert*] guidelines"), 454–55 ("the research presented herein clearly demonstrates the need for more science-based judicial education").

28. *See* Simon Locke, "The Public Understanding of Science—a Rhetorical Invention," 27 *Sci., Tech., and Hum. Values* 87 (2002) ("much of the debate in the field has focused on the validity of the so-called deficit model . . . . The term deficit reflects an expectation that members of the public are relatively ignorant of science and that these instruments help establish the extent of their knowledge deficit"); *see also* Mike Michael, "Comprehension, Apprehensions, Prehension: Heterogeneity and the Public Understanding of Science," 27 *Sci., Tech., and Hum. Values* 357, 359 (2002) (positivist, traditional orientation "has been criticized as deploying a deficit model").

29. *See* Mike Michael, "Ignoring Science: Discourses of Ignorance in the Public Understanding of Science," in *Misunderstanding Science? The Public Reconstruction of Science and Technology* (ed. Alan Irwin and Brian Wynne, 1996), at 109 (in recommendations "that there should be an increase in the amount and quality of science education," there is an implication that "science is the active disseminator and the fountain of meaning and agency, [and that] the public are merely the passive receivers and repositories"); *see also* Brian Wynne, "Misunderstood Misunderstandings: Social Identities and Public Uptake of Science," in *Misunderstanding Science? . . .* , *supra*, at 19 (discussing science as "cognitive content").

30. *See* Wynne, *supra* note 29, at 38.

31. *See* Mike Michael, "Ignoring Science . . . ," *supra* note 29, at 119–20; Wynne, *supra* note 29, at 26.

32. *See* Gatowski et al., *supra* note 24, at 438–41.

33. *Id.* at 441.

34. *See* Michael Mulkay and Nigel Gilbert, "Putting Philosophy to Work: Karl Popper's Influence on Scientific Practice," 11 *Phil. Soc. Sci.* 389, 398 (1981):

[A]ssessments of conformity to Popper's basic rule of scientific method hinge on scientists' interpretation of the term "falsification," and the meaning of "falsification" depends *entirely* on researchers' technical and scientific judgments. In situations of scientific uncertainty these judgments, and hence the meaning of Popperian rules, will be variable. Consequently, when there is uncertainty, the Popperian rules cannot provide a straightforward guide for scientists' actions or decisions. There is a gap between the rule and particular action which can only be bridged by the very scientific choice which the rule is intended to constrain.

In another formulation, the

> generality of the Popperian rules [like the falsification criterion], their lack of interpretive particularization and their independence of institutionalized social relationships, allow individual scientists considerable freedom to conceive of their own actions as Popperian in character and to attribute their intellectual success to the effectiveness of the Popperian approach.

Id. at 407.

As to the uses and misuses of Popper's falsifiability criterion in law, *see generally* Gary Edmond and David Mercer, "Conjectures and Exhumations: Citations of History, Philosophy and Sociology of Science in US Federal Courts," 14 *Law and Lit.* 309 (2002).

> What we . . . wish to emphasize is the degree of confidence invested by the [*Daubert*] majority in their Popperian inspired model of *the* scientific method [namely, the falsification criterion] and the absence, not only of conflicting and critical readings of Popper but of other philosophers and sociologists of science.

Id. at 313.

35. "Much of the cognitive research on scientific thinking has focused on particular cognitive activities such as falsification of hypotheses and noted that even scientists often fail to reason in a normatively correct manner (that is assuming the norms are correct!)" Kevin N. Dunbar, "Understanding the Role of Cognition in Science: The *Science as Category* Framework," in *The Cognitive Basis of Science* (ed. Peter Carruthers, Stephen Stich, and Michael Siegal, 2002), at 165.

36. *See, e.g.,* Gilles Fauconnier and Mark Turner, *The Way We Think: Conceptual Blending and the Mind's Hidden Complexities* 21 (2002):

> Most motions the skier can imagine are impossible or undesirable to execute. But within the conceptual blend prompted by the instructor [e.g., "pushing off," "skating," or "carrying a tray"], and under the conditions afforded by the environment, the desired motion will be emergent.

See also Steven L. Winter, *A Clearing in the Forest: Law, Life, and Mind* 3 (2001):

> Much of what we know is at the level of tacit knowledge. We can ride bicycles, compose new sentences, and make complex judgements about all sorts of everyday things without conscious effort or thought.

37. Neil B. Cohen, "The Gatekeeping Role in Civil Litigation and the Abdication of Legal Values in Favor of Scientific Values," 33 *Seton Hall L. Rev.* 943, 960 (2003).

38. *Id.* at 961.

39. *See id.* at 949 ("Science . . . routinely uses filters that prevent its experts from reaching exactly the sort of opinions . . . that should be utilized in a civil trial . . . ").

40. The research concerning jurors' understanding of burden of proof is inconclusive. It suggests, however, that the preponderance of evidence burden of proof is not

understood in the way that law professors often suggest, that is, as a 51 percent likelihood. *See generally* Joel D. Lieberman and Bruce D. Sales, "What Social Science Teaches Us about the Jury Instruction Process," 3 *Psychol., Pub. Pol'y., and L.* 589 (Dec. 1997); Rita James Simon and Linda Mahin, "Quantifying Burdens of Proof: A View from the Bench, the Jury, and the Classroom," 5 *Law and Soc'y. Rev.* 319 (1971).

41. *See* Cohen, *supra* note 37, at 949, 962.

42. James M. Shellow, "The Limits of Cross-Examination," 34 *Seton Hall L. Rev.* 317, 319 (2003).

43. Mansfield, *supra* note 16, at 82.

44. Edmond and Mercer, *supra* note 18, and 1, 3–4.

45. *Id.* at para. 9.

46. *Id.* at para. 16 ("Any simple linkage between science and practice is . . . undermined when we consider the reworking and simplification of scientific knowledge as it moves from abstract theorizing into standardized forms sufficient to fulfill a technological function"); *id.* at para. 23 ("Unlike the impression conveyed by junk science model proponents, in actuality scientists frequently find themselves in a competitive environment where strong emotional commitment to their views and sensitivity to finance and funding are essential to career progression—even academic and institutional survival"); *id.* at para. 25–26 (citing Michael Mulkay, *Science and the Sociology of Knowledge* 64 (1979)); *id.* at para. 28–29 ("Standards of proof, models, acceptable error rates, and observation . . . vary substantially from one branch of science to the next").

47. *See* Margaret A. Berger, "Expert Testimony in Criminal Proceedings: Questions *Daubert* Does Not Answer," 33 *Seton Hall L. Rev.* 1125, 1126 (2003).

48. *Id.* at 1126–29.

49. *Id.* at 1140.

50. Paul Giannelli, "The Supreme Court's 'Criminal' *Daubert* Cases," 33 *Seton Hall L. Rev.* 1071, 1107 (2003) (quoting Barry Scheck et al., *Actual Innocence: Five Days to Execution and Other Dispatches from the Wrongly Convicted* 146 (2000)).

51. *Id.* at 1108 (citing the Office of the Inspector General, United States Department of Justice, *The FBI Laboratory: An Investigation into Laboratory Practices and Alleged Misconduct in Explosives-Related and Other Cases* (1997)).

52. *See* Christopher Slobogin, "The Structure of Expertise in Criminal Cases," 34 *Seton Hall L. Rev.* 105, 108–16 (2003).

53. *Id.* at 117.

54. *Id.*

55. Moreover, while Slobogin comes close to idealizing the "positivistic" hard sciences by his repetitive contrast to the "socially constructed" soft sciences, he is actually a critic of strict reliability standards. Slobogin maintains that the standards lead to unfairness (toward criminal defendants) and to less-reliable outcomes because less-than-ideal science is better than no defense-oriented science at all. *See id.* at 118.

56. *See* Christoper B. Mueller, "*Daubert* Asks the Right Questions: Now Appellate Courts Should Help Find the Right Answers," 33 *Seton Hall L. Rev.* 987, 1019–22 (2003).

57. *See id.* at 1020–21.

58. *See* Mansfield, *supra* note 16, at 78–84.

59. *See id.* at 82–83.

60. *See id.* at 86 (citing Allen, *supra* note 4, at 7).

61. *See* David L. Faigman, "Expert Evidence in Flatland: The Geometry of a World without Scientific Culture," 34 *Seton Hall L. Rev.* 255, 264–65 (2003).

62. *Id.* at 256–58, 267.

63. *Id.* at 261–62.

64. *Id.* at 264, 267.

65. Comment 8, Rule 3.3, *ABA Model Rules of Professional Conduct* (2002).

66. *See* Jack B. Weinstein, "Improving Expert Testimony," 20 *Univ. Richmond L. Rev.* 473, 482 (1986) ("An expert can be found to testify to the truth of almost any factual theory, no matter how frivolous . . . . At the trial itself, an expert's testimony can be used to obfuscate what would otherwise be a simple case").

67. *See generally* Stephanie Francis Cahill, "Corporate-Fraud Law Forces Lawyers to be Whistle-Blowers," 1 *ABA Journal E-Report*, August 2, 2002 (Issue 29) (discussing Sarbanes-Oxley Act of 2002 requiring attorneys to report evidence of a material violation of securities law or a breach of fiduciary duty to general counsel or CEO); Diane Karpman, "New Law Turns Lawyers into Informants," *Calif. Bar J.*, Sept. 2002, at 23 (criticizing the Sarbanes-Oxley Act of 2002 as a federalization of ethics rules). Regarding the fall of Enron, *see* Peter Behr and April Witt, "Concerns Grow amid Conflicts," *Wash. Post*, July 30, 2002, at A1, A8 (criticizing outside counsel for not recommending further investigation).

68. *See generally* Peter W. Huber, *Galileo's Revenge: Junk Science in the Courtroom* (1991) (blaming judges, supposed experts, and also personal injury attorneys for junk science).

69. *See* Comment 1, Rule 3.3, *ABA Model Rules of Professional Conduct* (1983) (emphasis added):

> The advocate's task is to present the client's case with persuasive force. Performance of that duty . . . is qualified by the . . . duty of candor to the tribunal. *However, an advocate does not vouch for the evidence submitted in a cause; the tribunal is responsible for assessing its probative value.*

Our identification of this aphorism as relatively extreme is corroborated by the substantial revisions of that comment in the 2002 version of the *ABA Rules of Professional Conduct*, wherein "the task" becomes "an obligation," the "however" (suggesting an exception to the duty of candor) becomes "consequently," and the seeming exoneration from responsibility becomes a duty to ensure that the tribunal is not misled:

> . . . A lawyer . . . has an obligation to present the client's case with persuasive force. Performance of that duty . . . is qualified by the . . . duty of candor to the tribunal. Consequently, although a lawyer . . . is not required to . . . vouch for the evidence submitted in a cause, *the lawyer must not allow the tribunal to be misled by evidence that the lawyer knows to be false.*

Comment 1, Rule 3.3, *ABA Model Rules of Professional Conduct* (2002) (emphasis added). However, the spirit of the earlier comment is preserved, since Rule 3.3 still, indirectly if not clearly, allows an attorney to present evidence reasonably *believed*, but not *known*, to be false. Rule 3.3(a)(3), *ABA Model Rules of Professional Conduct* (2002) (". . . A Lawyer may refuse to offer evidence . . . that the lawyer reasonably believes is false").

70. *See, e.g.,* Dick Thornburgh, "Junk Science—the Lawyer's Ethical Responsibilities," 25 *Fordham Urb. L. J.* 449, 449 (1998).

71. Steven Lubet, *Expert Testimony: A Guide for Expert Witnesses and the Lawyers Who Examine Them* 171 (1998).

72. That is, "without necessarily believing the view is correct" is seemingly preferred to "even if she believes that the view is false."

73. Rule 3.3(a)(3), *ABA Model Rules of Professional Conduct* (2002) (emphasis added). "Offering such proof may reflect adversely on the lawyer's ability to discriminate in the quality of evidence and thus impair the lawyer's effectiveness as an advocate." *Id.*, Comment 9.

74. *See* Rule 3.3(a)(3), *ABA Model Rules of Professional Conduct, supra* note 69.

75. *See* Virginia L.E.O. 1650 (9/8/95).

76. Comment 8, Rule 3.3, *ABA Model Rules of Professional Conduct, supra* note 64; *see also id.*, Rule 1.0(f) ("A person's knowledge can be inferred from circumstances").

77. *See* Comment 8, Rule 3.3, *supra* note 65.

78. *See* Geoffrey C. Hazard Jr. and W. William Hodes, *The Law of Lawyering: A Handbook on the Model Rules of Professional Conduct* § 3.3:401 (2d ed., 1992 Supp.) (emphasis added) ("If the lawyer's uncertainty is genuine and reasonable, he can present the evidence without risk of violating Rule 3.3").

79. 750 F2d. at 1501 (11th Cir. 1985), recons'd at 866 F.2d 1303 (11th Cir. 1989).

80. 750 F.2d at 1503.

81. 750 F.2d at 1503 (emphasis added).

82. 750 F.2d at 1505.

83. 878 F. Supp. at 986 (S.D. Tex 1995).

84. 878 F. Supp. at 990–91.

85. *See* Virginia L.E.O. 1687 (8/24/92).

86. *See* Note, Justin P. Murphy, "Expert Witnesses at Trial: Where Are the Ethics?" 14 *Geo. J. Legal Ethics* 217, 230 (2000).

87. Weinstein, *supra* note 66, at 491.

88. *See* Fed. R. Evid. 702.

89. *See, e.g., Goebel v. Denver and Rio Grande Western Railroad Co.*, 215 F.3d 1083, 1086–88 (10th Cir. 2000) (admitting doctor's testimony was abuse of discretion; court should have "vigilantly" made detailed findings and "carefully and meticulously" reviewed the evidence).

90. *See* Thornburgh, *supra* note 70, at 449.

91. *Id.* at 462, citing DR 7-102, *ABA Model Code of Professional Responsibility* (1981) (duty to represent a client within the bounds of the law).

92. *See* Rule 3.1, *ABA Model Rules of Professional Conduct* (2002).

93. *See* Thornburgh, *supra* note 70, at 463.

94. *See id.* at 467, citing *Fed. R. Civ. P.* 11. It "is arguable that Rule 11 is violated by an attorney who files a complaint which is based entirely on junk science." *Id.*, n.106.

95. *See* Thornburgh, *supra* note 70, at 467, 469.

96. *See id.* at 463–64, discussing the difficulty of applying *Daubert* standards: "Even the Supreme Court in *Daubert* admitted that, 'shaky' scientific evidence could still be admissible." *Id.* at 463, citing *Daubert*, 509 U.S. at 596.

97. *See* Thornburgh, *supra* note 70, at 468.

98. *See id.* at 449 (breast implant litigation in the face of contrary, reliable epidemiological data; Bendectin litigation despite lack of causal connection with birth defects; Norplant litigation despite FDA and physicians groups insisting it is safe).

99. *See id.* at 462, 469.

100. *See* Thornburgh, *supra* note 70, at 466.

101. Sheila Jasanoff, "Hidden Experts: Judging Science after *Daubert*," in *Trying Times: Science and Responsibilities after* Daubert (ed. Vivian Weil, 2001), at 45.

102. *See generally* Mansfield, *supra* note 16.

103. *See* R. Erik Lillquist, "A Comment on the Admissibility of Forensic Evidence," 33 *Seton Hall L. Rev.* 1189, 1203–4 (2003).

104. *See* Stephen Breyer, *Breaking the Vicious Circle: Toward Effective Risk Regulation* 59–72 (1993).

Chapter Five

Science *Is* a Pragmatic Activity

LISTENING TO CONVERSATIONS ABOUT SCIENCE

What do lawyers and scientists talk about when they talk about science? To find out, it will not do to examine what they say while on vacation, when nothing turns on the debate. One must find conversations wherein lawyers and scientists are engaged with concrete problems.

We begin this chapter by considering the pretrial depositions of scientists in recent tobacco litigation. (The customary procedure is for the lawyers on both sides to meet with a witness in a law office. During this meeting, the witness testifies under oath, and a stenographer records and then transcribes the testimony. The transcripts are used by the lawyers to prepare for trial.) What lawyers and scientists say during depositions is serious talk, since what is said may determine whether (or how much) money moves from the defendant's pocket into the plaintiff's pocket. In these depositions, one would expect the focus to be on technical matters, but both lawyers and scientists move back and forth between naturalistic frames of reference and decidedly social explanations of how scientific knowledge is produced. Sometimes the conversation is technical and methodological, but lawyers and scientists also talk about funding and economics, credibility and community consensus, historically evolving standards in various scientific disciplines, and even philosophical presuppositions. Both naturalistic and social forms of explanation can be seen to involve negative and positive aspects of science: mistakes are made on the technical *and* social side of things, but progress is also explainable due to technical *and* social factors.

In science studies, sometimes called the sociology of scientific knowledge, investigators often visit laboratories to observe what scientists say and do.

Their work is analogous to anthropologists engaging in ethnography when they visit a foreign culture to figure out its cultural practices and values. One might even say that lawyers, in depositions of scientists, behave like ethnographers, visiting a tribe that is foreign to them—they tend to ask about how the "natives" produce their culture of scientific knowledge.

Following our analysis of the depositions below, we discuss our own ethnographic study of three neuroscientists, which interviews reveal the same patterns of discourse that we found in the depositions. Throughout this chapter, we draw analogies between science studies and the use of science in law.

SOCIOTECHNICAL ARGUMENTS IN SCIENTIFIC DISCOURSE

> The analysis of the argumentation and rhetoric of scientists during the [*Hybritech Inc. v. Monoclonal Antibodies, Inc.*] patent trial is more than a discussion of "literary devices" . . . . The problems raised during the proceedings and the solutions proposed by expert witnesses were grounded in a seamless web of philosophical, economic, and social distinctions . . . . [E]xpert witnesses used tools that do not differ, in principle, from tools mobilized by philosophers, economists and sociologists when constructing representations of "society."[1]

Over fifteen years ago, three Canadian scholars published a unique study of scientific expertise in a U.S. courtroom.[2] Drawing upon "recent work in the sociology of science," the authors demonstrated that "while one might expect 'technical' arguments to play a central role in patent litigation proceedings, 'social,' 'historical,' 'economic,' or 'philosophical' arguments were coextensive with and constitutive of the 'technical.'"[3] They concluded that the "interaction between legal and scientific categories" should not be "viewed as a clash between 'hard scientific facts' and legal conventions or representations, but as a back-and-forth movement between different kinds of representation."[4] In other words, we should not simply assume that scientists operate within a naturalistic framework that is sometimes translated into obviously social contexts: the courtroom, doctrinal categories, and legal discourse. Rather, the discourse of scientists themselves, whether in a laboratory or in a deposition, alternatively includes recourse to both naturalistic and social frameworks of explanation. Social, economic, historical, and philosophical arguments, *in addition to* technical arguments, are often mobilized for rhetorical advantages in scientific disputes—even those disputes that are internal to science and have nothing to do with litigation.

By way of contrast, the recourse to social explanations in depositions or cross-examination of scientific experts often represents an effort to discredit or criticize a scientific argument. For example, manuals on expert testimony often recommend attacking a scientist for some bias, interest, or motivation that interfered with the scientist's pretended methodological rigor. Several studies of examinations of scientific experts—one using actual trial transcripts—demonstrate techniques to establish how, in a particular case, human judgment or communal practices got in the way of scientific judgment and practices.[5] In effect, social frameworks of explanation are associated with disclosing bad science, just as naturalistic frameworks of explanation are associated with good science. In conventional legal discourse, therefore, there seems to be little recognition either (i) that scientists themselves mobilize both naturalistic and social frameworks in their arguments, or (ii) that lawyers, sometimes unwittingly, use social frameworks of explanation to bolster their scientific arguments rather than as a tool to discredit opposing arguments.

The Construction of Sociotechnical Identities in a Patent Dispute

Hybritech v. Monoclonal Antibodies, Inc. involved a claim by Hybritech that the defendant infringed upon a Hybritech patent for an immunological diagnostic test kit that detected or measured the presence of a given antigen in body fluids.[6] The defendant, to establish prior art and to invalidate the patent, claimed that Hybritech's diagnostic kit was simply based on techniques used by immunologists before Hybritech's patent was filed.[7] Specifically, the defendant argued that the differences between the techniques used in earlier experiments and the immunoassay techniques involved in the Hybritech kit were insignificant. Hybritech's claim relied on a strong distinction between the two. On this point, the federal district court agreed with the defendant, but its decision was reversed and remanded on appeal in favor of Hybritech.

In their study of *Hybritech*, Professors Alberto Cambrosio, Peter Keating, and Michael Mackenzie focused on the expert scientific testimony in the case. They distinguished, at the outset, between the legal and scientific discourses at the trial. For example, the distinction between and ambiguities surrounding immunological techniques were said to be "extant in scientific practice," and were not inventions of law.[8] On the other hand, legal protection of Hybritech's patent required inter alia that Hybritech's invention be non-obvious to those skilled in the art, and novel in terms of prior art.

> [T]he "key issue" according to the [trial and appellate courts] was "whether the defendant [had] overcome the presumption of non-obviousness . . . . [I]n order to demonstrate novelty and non-obviousness, the patent holder must demonstrate non-identity *and* discontinuity. [The defendant must show] continuity *or* identity.[9]

Hence the authors' reference, in their subtitle, to "Construction of Sociotechnical Identities," because "questions of identity engender not only arguments
about what counts as 'the same,' but also, about what belongs in the 'same
category' . . . ."[10] Criteria of identity, the authors argued, are both technical
and social, and rely on rhetoric and representations not found in nature.[11]

Dr. Herzenberg, a witness for the defense in *Hybritech*, doubted any "big
distinction" between the techniques used before the Hybritech patent was
filed and those used in the Hybritech diagnostic kit.[12] Herzenberg's trivial-
ization of the distinction claimed by Hybritech was an attempt to push "those
invoking it to the margins of science," but on cross-examination,
"Hybritech's lawyer was able to use that move to redefine the relevant do-
main of expertise to exclude Herzenberg":

> Q. [Y]ou are not an expert in the field of developing commercially useful im-
> munoassays; isn't that right?
>
> A. Well, there are some commercially very useful immunoassays which I have
> had a bit to do with developing. There are others I haven't.
>
> Q. You are not a leader in the field of immunoassays; isn't that right?
>
> A. Of the kind of immunoassays that I believe you would consider in that par-
> ticular field, I am not.[13]

As to the legal category of "non-obvious . . . for any person of ordinary skill
in the art," the term *person* seems to have been, in this litigation, translated
into *social world*—the trial judge viewed the invention as obvious "to those
in the scientific and commercial world." But Hybritech's experts helped distinguish between the "social world of pure science [and] the social world of
developers of commercial immunoassays," the latter of which became the
real world where the appellate panel found "non-obviousness."[14] That distinction became significant for Hybritech's characterization of Herzenberg's
work as "theoretical, if not esoteric," and "far beyond the realm of clinical or
commercial reality."[15]

In the *Hybritech* litigation, supposedly universal scientific concepts and
definitions were challenged by Hybritech's proposed "opposition between academic and commercial science."[16] Science and industry, that is, appeared
"not as a priori entities . . . but as the result of contingent constructs or rhetorical resources within an agonistic field."[17] Another witness, Hybritech's chief
executive officer, "managed to dissolve the logical identity [between earlier
experimental techniques and Hybritech's diagnostic kit] into an historical dis-
continuity" when he stated:

> *We developed, over a period of time, the practice that they were distinctive
> enough procedures that we should use two different terms. And I suspect many*

immunologists today would make the distinction . . . I didn't really understand the significance of the difference . . . until I really started getting involved in depth at Hybritech.[18]

Even Gary David, Hybritech's senior scientist, conceded in his testimony that he "may well have been and was in fact one of those individuals [who in the past] did not distinguish between" Hybritech's procedures and earlier experiments.[19] The defendant's assertion of the identity of earlier techniques and Hybritech's "invention" was thereby characterized as anachronistic.

Indeed, the conflict between Hybritech and Monoclonal Antibodies, which was reflected in the conflicting judicial opinions that resulted, can roughly be understood as a conflict between two views of science (even though the proponents on both sides of the conflict at times seemed to rely alternatively on both views). The defendant and the trial judge relied on a naturalistic (rather than social or historical) representation of Hybritech's activities, for while the process of discovery was certainly historical, the objects of discovery were ahistorical, natural entities. Hybritech's experts, on the other hand, repeatedly contextualized the natural objects or entities in immunology. For example, Herzenberg emphasized the chemistry and biology that were there all along, while Hybritech's experts claimed the invention was "the diagnostic kit as a package and not . . . its individual components." Likewise, when the defendant characterized "Hybritech's supposed innovation [as a] mere substitution . . . of their own [components for similar components used in Abbott Labs' diagnostic kit]," Gary David introduced the notion that the seemingly direct substitution was indirect, or only obvious in retrospect.[20]

> First, [the difference between direct and indirect substitution] was announced in terms of the psychological difference between knowing that one was making a substitution and thinking that one was making an improvement or inventive step . . . . In other words, to appreciate what Hybritech had done, it was necessary to understand what they thought they were doing.
> A related argument [stressed] the "inherent uncertainty" involved in dealing with "natural systems" . . . . [O]ne could not know in advance what variables were relevant to the behavior of a natural system.[21]

Moreover, while the substitution may have been obvious to lay immunologists, those working at the molecular level "have a much clearer picture," and "the substitution [for the latter group] appeared neither obvious nor easy,"[22] even if it was "reasonable, logical to try to do it."[23] Finally,

> another Hybritech witness, Alfred Nisonoff, a well known immunologist . . . and author of a standard . . . textbook, [testified that] the substitution . . . was novel when viewed from an historical perspective. When Hybritech began its research

in 1979, . . . it was generally believed that [Hybritech's particular substitution would not] have much commercial use . . . .[24]

Cambrosio et al. thereby highlight the social, rather than natural, framework of Hybritech's experts' representations: from a historical perspective, "it was . . . not self-evident to use" immunological techniques as Hybritech did, and in synchronic terms, a social distinction was introduced between lay immunologists and those "who would have a much clearer picture . . . because of their orientation, their experience."[25]

In other words, by resorting to a social framework the distinction between the social and the technical was increasingly blurred, the social presenting itself as constitutive of the technical, and vice-versa.[26]

Even the defendant's representations unwittingly shifted to a social framework at times, as when Herzenberg referred to Hybritech's innovation as being limited to the commercial world.[27]

Establishing priority in a patent trial also "requires identifying an entity as novel"—that is, as distinguishable, as an autonomous entity—which task "involves constructing identity criteria for the object in question."[28] For Cambrosio et al.,

much of the debate over the identity of technical objects was expressed in terms of the classification of technosocial units such as specialties and in terms of temporal discontinuities. For example, whether [Hybritech's technique was innovative] depended on where and when you did your work, and not on what it was you did. In other words, what one did could not be accounted for independently of the context. The different contexts, in turn, gave rise to differing interpretations of the degree to which human manipulation of "natural" entities may reorganize [them such] that they acquire a new identity . . . .[29]

In the end, on appeal, the defendant's focus on universality, consistency, and ahistorical natural entities gave way to Hybritech's technosocial world of constitutive interventions, incommensurable theories, and commercial fate.

It bears mention that the analytical and terminological frameworks used by Cambrosio et al. were not used or implied by the judges in the trial and appellate opinions in *Hybritech*, or even in the expert testimony in court. Rather, a unique template—a "third way" of interpretation—is imposed by Cambrosio et al. on the scientific testimony in order both to elucidate the dispute and to offer an explanation for the strikingly different assessments of the patent's validity by the trial judge and the appellate opinion's author. Both judicial opinions are highly technical or naturalistic in their introductory accounts of immunology as well as in their application of legal categories. No mention is made of social or historical contexts, the rhetorical aspects of scientific discovery, or even the economic forces driving science (except insofar as the appellate opinion discusses Hybritech's success in the market as a marker of the validity of its patent). Indeed, a more conventional legal analysis of the *Hybritech* dispute might focus on the (unfortunate) fact that the district court (unfairly) adopted the defendant's *pretrial* brief, and its *pretrial* findings of facts and conclusions of law "virtually verbatim" and without "supporting evidence."[30] The trial judge simply could not see any innovation in Hybritech's diagnostic kit, and all of the advantages exploited by Hybritech, which were obvious due to the "inherent, known, and expected properties of" natural entities, could be accounted for as clever marketing skills.[31] For the appellate panel, it was *just as clear* that no other researchers knew or did precisely what Hybritech knew and did, which is why Hybritech's kit worked and succeeded in the marketplace.[32] Instead of explaining which court was correct in its application of patent law, Cambrosio et al. explain (i) how the trial judge could have seen Hybritech's alleged invention as a minor and insignificant realization of what naturally flows from known elements and processes—a naturalistic framework—and (ii) how the appellate panel could have seen Hybritech's innovations in a framework of social, historical, rhetorical, and economic *contexts*. Again, even that insight could be restated in terms of superb lawyering, but the analysis of Cambrosio et al. specifically addresses the constructive accounts of scientists themselves not simply under the guidance of lawyers, but in their typical scientific discourse. Scientists themselves regularly judge their work to be novel, routine, or some combination of these. Observing how scientific talk about novelty interacts with legal talk about novelty is daunting. Cambrosio et al. have not said the last word, but they made a good start. We believe that recourse to rhetorical strategies and appeals to social subgroups or historical contexts—both mergers of the social and the technical—appear in other scientific fields.

We next explore a dispute belonging to the field of tobacco litigation, where certain legal issues are similar to those in patent cases insofar as they involve what scientists working for tobacco companies *knew*. As in *Hybritech*, perception often depends on where the scientist was, what the scientist was thinking, and what the scientist thought he or she was thinking. The objects of nature and what naturally flows from one's knowledge of them are not obvious, or more accurately, what *is* obvious depends on social, historical, and economic contexts that every scientist does not share.

Sociotechnical Arguments in Tobacco Litigation

Labelle v. Philip Morris Incorporated involved a claim (by the personal representative of a deceased smoker's estate) against various cigarette manufacturers for damages on the basis of strict product liability, unfair trade practices, negligence or gross negligence, and civil conspiracy. Philip Morris moved for summary judgment, which was granted inter alia on the basis that the plaintiff had not established a design defect showing that cigarettes were unreasonably dangerous.[33] One of the many issues in the case was whether the plaintiff could show that "a safer alternative design for [defendant's] cigarettes existed," and the plaintiff offered the deposition testimony of Dr. William Farone, describing "several technologies that Philip Morris could have employed to reduce the dangers of its cigarettes." Farone's testimony was excluded under *Daubert* standards because his hypothesis, that safer alternatives existed, had not been tested by him or by Philip Morris.[34]

Focusing on the alternative design for a safer cigarette as the object of inquiry for Dr. Farone, a brief review of his deposition predictably reveals that he primarily employs a naturalistic framework to show its existence. Significantly, however, Farone alternatively uses naturalistic *and* social frameworks—strategically and rhetorically—in his accounts of his scientific activities. Likewise, the attorney deposing Farone shifts back and forth between naturalistic and social frameworks of explanation, for purposes of discrediting Farone or challenging his testimony. Our own analysis of the deposition is not concerned with the accuracy of Farone's testimony; moreover, we neither take a position concerning the outcome of the litigation, nor wish to criticize either Farone or Philip Morris counsel for their explanations. Rather, we wish to show how recourse to naturalistic and social frames of reference are typical in scientific discourse because science is both naturalistic and social.

Counsel for Philip Morris began his deposition of Dr. Farone by asking if he "intended to offer any expert opinions on the subject of alternative designs of cigarettes," and Farone replied, "Yes . . . . That it is possible to make safer cigarettes, that the means for doing so was known . . . ."[35] Asked about the code of ethics for chemistry, one of Farone's specialties, Farone said he would offer an opinion "that Philip Morris has not conducted itself according to this Code of Conduct."[36]

Q. Okay, and did you ever express to any of your superiors in writing that you thought that the conduct of the company's business was being done unethically?

A. I don't recall whether I . . . . [R]ather than send a memo . . . or something like that, that's not necessarily going to get the job done, okay? The better way to do it in a society like we have is that you work within the confines of that society to work with the people to try to change their opinion about how they do business . . . .[37]

Immediately, not only is the social aspect of proper science as an *ethical* practice evoked, but society generally is represented as confining what scientists can do and how they can best communicate their insights.

Because of his published accusation that the tobacco industry "continues to provide erroneous results to the public,"[38] Farone was asked whether he meant

anything other than that the words are . . . wordsmithed in such a way that it leaves an impression that you think is inaccurate [e.g., that smoking "doesn't do you any harm or we really don't know . . . "]?

A. Oh, the results are wrong also . . . . The results that are presented are incorrectly presented. Results are results. It's just a question of how you paint them.

Q. You disagree with the interpretation of the data . . . ?

A. Interpretation of data and in some cases the means by which the data was . . . collected, the data that was selected, and the experiment that was done to prove the point.

Q. Okay . . . . Do you contend that the data is . . . falsified data?

A. That's tricky. The data isn't false. Data is data . . . . It's that the experiment is set up without enough information to be able to test the premise . . . .

Q. Okay. What you mean is that the conclusions drawn from the data, the way the experiment was set up . . . those could be done better, they were done in the wrong way?

A. They were selective. In other words, if you want to prove a result, you kind of doctor the experimental setup so that way you don't have to lie about the result.[39]

Farone is in this interchange both resisting the attorney's characterization of science as rhetorical, and also appealing to a naturalistic framework: results are results, and data are data. Scientific facts, that is, are not subject to "painting" or interpretation if the data are properly collected and the experiment is set up with enough information. While Farone had earlier referred to social aspects—ethical codes, rhetorical necessities—as integral to science, social aspects like influencing an experiment and wordsmithing are now aligned with bad science. From our vantage, of course, the distinction between good and bad social aspects is appropriate, just as one may distinguish between good and bad methodology.

Farone also testified that he resisted the strategy at Philip Morris to "poke holes" in studies that were critical of the tobacco industry, and that he recommended that the company create its own "hard data" to rebut critics.[40] Asked whether he had done so, Farone replied

I would love to do that. I need to have a budget to do that. If Philip Morris or one of the other people want to provide the money, I'd love to do it . . . . I don't have the resources to do that.[41]

This interchange became significant in the court's granting summary judgment to Philip Morris because Farone's hypothesis (that safer cigarettes were possible) had not been tested. For our purposes, the interchange exemplifies a strategic appeal to economic aspects of science—funding and resources—as integral to the production of hard facts.

To begin to lay the foundation for the argument that Farone's views had not been tested, Philip Morris counsel asked Farone about general scientific principles. Farone was first asked about falsifiability as the basis for scientific hypothesis, specifically whether

> a hypothesis can move . . . to being a theory and then a law, is that right?
>
> A. Correct.
>
> Q. [A]nd you conduct experiments to try to disprove the hypothesis, is that right?
>
> A. Correct.
>
> Q. And if the experiments don't . . . disprove the hypothesis, after a while it moves to become a theory and then law.
>
> A. Correct.
>
> Q. Okay . . . what happens [if a hypothesis is untestable]?[42]

This philosophical question could be important if Farone conceded that his hypothesis was not testable, since testability is a marker of science under *Daubert*. Farone seemed to know where counsel for Philip Morris was going, and was uncooperative:

> [Y]ou don't just formulate a hypothesis out of air . . . . [Y]ou go back and look at the premises . . . .
>
> For example, you could argue [about] the hypothesis that water . . . always flows downhill. It's untestable because you can't watch it forever . . . . But if we accept the laws of thermodynamics and the laws of gravity and a few other laws as being tested sufficiently that we believe in them, you can use . . . those laws to say, "Well, I can't disprove that theory . . . . I'm going to accept it even though I can't test it in every case."
>
> And as a matter of fact, one can argue that you can never completely test a hypothesis . . . .[43]

For obvious strategic reasons, Farone shifts from a naturalistic perspective to a social framework: some scientific hypotheses are not ultimately testable but are nevertheless widely accepted in the scientific community. The implication is that the truth of Farone's testimony regarding a safer cigarette design is a matter of consensus.

Philip Morris counsel then turned to a different question, which placed science in a social context by referring to decisions (among scientists) about what is worth researching, much the same way that Farone had referred to the need for economic resources to test a theory. Farone was asked about a testable hypothesis that

> is never actually tested by anybody, whether because it's not regarded as sufficiently worthwhile of spending time and effort to test it or for any other reason? Does that hypothesis . . . progress inexorably toward becoming a theory and a law of science?
>
> A. Yes . . . and the reason is because . . . . [I]t's testable [and] it may be so accepted already that it isn't worth testing . . . [or perhaps it isn't tested because] I don't want to have the evidence that Marlboro causes cancer . . . .
>
> Q. . . . Now you'll admit that one possibility is also that [the] hypothesis is so out to lunch, I don't want to waste my time even thinking about it, isn't that right? . . .
>
> A. Of course, but the point is there's usually a reason why they don't want to do it . . . .
>
> Q. [I]sn't your testimony that we determine whether it's true or false by . . . testing it, right?
>
> A. Right.
>
> Q. And if you don't test it, how do you know?
>
> A. No, no . . . you're missing the point. If you don't test it, you can't prove it's wrong, and if that hypothesis is based on fundamental good science and observation, . . . that's it. That is accepted.[44]

Farone, in the off-the-cuff and informal setting of the deposition, anchors his picture of science as seemingly speculative—that is, in his acceptance of untested hypotheses—in the body of fundamental good science and observation, which is a naturalistic reference. The social aspect of research decisions is then associated with bad science: "You can always argue that the reason why . . . Philip Morris didn't do the testing of Marlboro versus Merit is because all 250 scientists at Philip Morris decided it wasn't worth testing."[45] In other words, Farone does not "take the bait" that science obviously proceeds on the basis of *social* decisions as to what is worth researching, and recharacterizes the decisions of scientists to forego research as either good (the answer is already known) or bad (the scientist doesn't want to know the answer), while the inevitable social determinant of what is worth testing, an aspect of all scientific inquiry, disappears from his argument. Farone's strategy at this point is understandable, and while we believe that science does proceed on the basis of social decisions, we are not criticizing Farone for his resistance to his inquisitor. Our point, throughout this analysis, is simply to show that historical, social, rhetorical, and economic aspects of science co-exist with technical and methodological aspects, and that certain aspects of science are alternatively emphasized and deemphasized, for strategic and rhetorical reasons, in the heat of the battle that is called a deposition.

Turning to the notion of a "cancer score," described by Farone as the result of "tests by which one can determine whether something is carcinogenic . . . ,"[46] Philip Morris counsel continued:

> Is there anything out there that stops the government or researchers outside of the [tobacco] companies from figuring out a methodology to . . . come up with what you have described as a cancer score?
>
> A. Oh, of course there is . . . . The tobacco industry . . . [W]hen the FDA wanted to regulate tobacco, the industry goes to court and kills it. When the EPA wants to [regulate] secondhand smoke, [the tobacco industry tries] to fight it in court. So the industry is the only thing that's holding up the development of these scores . . . .
>
> The only reason why it hasn't been done is because—and I was there . . . they didn't want to know the answer . . . .
>
> Q. [I]s there anything that prevents any researcher [from] coming up with a score on their own?
>
> A. Yes . . . . Two things. One is the resources and the funds to do that . . . which the industry has . . . .
>
> And the second thing is the opposition of the industry . . . the industry would only cooperate and be involved [if their brand names were not used].[47]

Here the social influence on science is initially represented pejoratively, by reference to the industry as a barrier to scientific research. Yet when Farone is challenged to explain why scientists have not developed cancer scores, he shifts to a social framework wherein the cooperation of the industry and its financial resources are necessary elements of good science. Indeed, the social framework of consensus-building techniques among scientists is presented by Farone in a positive light:

> Q. . . . Wouldn't it be conceivable that some scientists [testing for a cancer score] . . . might say, "Well, I think you ought to weigh mouse skin [test results] more heavily than [others]." Other scientists might say something different, right?
>
> A. Right . . . .

Q. Okay. What's the mechanism by which we should come to a consensus . . . ?

A. Science has that mechanism already built in. Each of those scientists who have those opinions publish their reasons, they publish data . . . , and then those different opinions are compared to the epidemiology.[48]

Farone here shifts back to a naturalistic framework, arguing that consensus is anchored in published data. But Philip Morris counsel then challenges Farone's naturalistic framework because of the current "environment":

If you were honest, you'd know that in this environment, if Philip Morris put out its own score, then people . . . like yourself who testify against the companies would say, "It's wrong. It's designed to be misleading." Isn't that right?[49]

Isn't scientific discourse, in other words, structured by a particular context? Not surprisingly, Farone does not concede that point in the antagonistic setting of a deposition. Farone therefore answers no, because the tobacco industry could submit data to a neutral "regulating agency" to do the testing:

[N]obody prevents the industry from going back to Congress and say[ing], "Look, because we have this problem, we want to be regulated so we can come to some closure . . . ."

Q. Dr. Farone, put yourself back . . . in the shoes you were wearing at Philip Morris when you were part of the company. Don't you think the company needs there to be a consensus about the appropriate way to weight these various assays before doing anything?[50]

Once again, counsel for Philip Morris is insisting that science is in part a social activity—controversies require consensus, which implies the presence of consensus-building techniques and negotiation. And again, Farone balks because coming up with a score is a naturalistic endeavor: "I think . . . the industry should take the lead and come up with a score and then take the criticism."[51] But then Farone concedes that there are social and contextual *reasons* to do this, because it is

the most responsible thing to do. It also reduces . . . liability, OK? So it's responsible, good citizenship, follows the Code of Conduct. It's good business.[52]

Asked what one does when various tests have varying results, Farone suggested that

if you have seven tests . . . you are going to have some anomalies, but when you in fact average those, you're still going to get a direction in which to head, and then if you follow it up with brand-specific epidemiology, you've done your best . . . .

Q. Doesn't the outcome of that decision . . . depend on how you decide to weight the various assays?

A. Yes, but if you have seven of them [you might not weight the anomaly very high] . . . .

Q. Let's say it's three [anomalies].

A. Out of how many?

Q. Seven . . . .

A. Well, it's still okay.

Q. Okay.

A. Because I think we know sort of the answer from epidemiology.

Q. . . . Have any epidemiologists published . . . peer-reviewed articles . . . that come to the same conclusion as you . . . ?

A. No, because we're just getting around to that . . . .

[Y]ou have to adapt the kinds of market analysis techniques that . . . some of these other studies use . . . . So you have to have some pretty decent agreement to do that . . . .[53]

Here it is Farone explicating social context and consensus-building techniques as a way to explain the basis of secure scientific knowledge. Even testing, that is, always involves some communal judgments. For example, when Farone was at Lever Brothers, scientists

were trying to determine whether we should put [a certain chemical] in detergent products. So you go through a battery of tests, including three-year carcinogenic studies, mutagenic studies, and you always have that problem. How long do I take the test? How long does it have to go? And you make the decision . . . based on your best scientific judgment, and you get a score and you can argue about what that means, but the point is you have a point of reference to then track the epidemiology, what happens.[54]

If the tests of a chemical indicate a problem, which is of course not a natural entity but rather a matter of judgment that is subject to debate, you're going to stop making that chemical. That's the deal.

And so you can always agree, given the desire to do so, on something that's rational with regard to these scores . . . .

Q. Okay, and your testimony is that the reason it hasn't happened by people outside the industry is because the industry has kept them from doing it . . . ?

A. No, . . . I gave you a bunch of reasons, okay? You've got to have the money, you've got to have the resources . . . .[55]

Farone's testimony is that Philip Morris had the resources but lacked the desire to discover the health risks of smoking: "Philip Morris knew exactly how to determine the carcinogenic potential of these things and elected not to do it."[56] Moreover, independent testing laboratories used "reference cigarettes" (rather than, say, Marlboros) to ensure standardized research, but those scientists, Farone explained, "want to be friends with the industry because [the industry is] trying to help them do stuff. So [they] go along with the program to a certain extent."[57] At this point, Farone's testimony is consistent with our own view of science: even though resources and rational agreement among scientists are conceded to be a social framework of good science, some social aspects of science—the industry's lack of desire and independent scientists' friendship with the industry—are represented as barriers to good science.

In the case of one new cigarette technology—a cobalt and aluminum filter—Seton Hall University was asked to evaluate the product independently. Asked about the university report that the product would "have no probability of success for reducing levels of carbon monoxide in conventional cigarettes," Farone replied that the test was flawed by using a plug filter. "I made [that filter] and we used it and . . . it works just fine . . . . [But] you can make one that you send off for evaluation that doesn't work to prove your point."[58] Having suggested that some researchers interfere with naturalistic experiments, Farone confirmed that inside Philip Morris, the

> people carry out good science . . . . So we're talking about the interpretation of that science and how it's set up to confuse and confound . . . .
>
> You know, once we're really clear on the ground rules and they agree to it, I think they'll do it. The problem is getting the agreement that that's what they need to do. You know, I'd have to sit down and . . . sketch it out and . . . we'd argue about it like all scientists do, and we'd agree on a protocol and they could carry it out.[59]

We are in agreement with Farone when the social framework returns in his testimony as necessary to good science: a community of scientists clarifies the ground rules, argues about experiments, and agrees on a protocol.

The hybrid character of scientific practice as a social and naturalistic activity is also clear in Farone's testimony in another design defect case, *Neri v. R.J. Reynolds Tobacco Company*, in which testimony was also (as in *Labelle*) found to be unreliable under *Daubert* standards.[60] Farone there also mobilized social explanations for the lack of both consensus and testing with respect to the availability of a safer, alternative cigarette design. Early in his deposition for *Neri*, Farone relied on a naturalistic framework of explanation:

> I can testify as to what cigarettes could have been made available that would have greatly reduced the probability of [plaintiff's] emphysema . . . .

Q. You were aware [when you were working at Philip Morris] that cigarettes were statistically associated with diseases; is that correct?

A. I was aware that cigarettes caused diseases . . . .

Q. And you believed that [cigarettes] caused emphysema?

A. I wouldn't characterize it as being a belief, but I'm saying scientifically on the basis of the evidence, I accepted the evidence as being non-refuted that cigarettes caused cancer, emphysema, yes . . . . Belief does not enter into science. We're not talking religion. So, I don't like use of the word "belief." Either there's evidence to support it and you accept it scientifically or you don't. . . .[61]

When his views are challenged as mere beliefs, Farone perhaps overreacts and exaggerates when he claims that belief "does not enter science." However, when R.J. Reynolds counsel asks a naturalistic question: "What is the pH level for Winston [brand cigarettes]?" Farone shifts to a contingent and conventional, rather than objective and certain, framework:

As you asked the question, I don't even know what you mean by the pH level . . . because you don't describe the protocol that I can use to measure it.

In other words, anything in science that you talk about has a measurement, the speed of something. There's an experimental method to measure it.

* * * *

[W]hat you have to . . . recognize [is] that no two of [the tobacco] companies did it exactly the same way.[62]

As R.J. Reynolds counsel continues to challenge Dr. Farone's failure to produce the results of a pH test, Farone actually rejects the lawyer's idealistic and naturalistic framework, including using pH as a natural entity, by introducing more social contingencies:

Q. How many times did you test the Winston product for pH?

A. I, personally?

Q. Yes.

A. [A] fellow working with me did it. We did it . . . for the competitive information reports at Philip Morris . . . .

The number that I'm recalling is from some of the competitive intelligence information using one or more of those protocols. The relevance of all of this has to do with the changes over time. So a single point in time pH does not mean too much.

* * * *

There's a lot of debate among the scientists as to which protocol is the most meaningful in terms of what happens during the combustion process.

Q. Did you consider the Cambridge [pad] method to be a reliable method of—

A. Let's distinguish between accuracy and precision. It's a precise method, that is, it's reproducible. [But] the accuracy of it in terms of nicotine delivery is debatable . . . .

Q. The pH measurement using the Cambridge pad method is an acceptable method . . . , though, in scientific circles?

A. Yes . . . . It has been used for a long time . . . . [But] you can cheat or fudge on that measurement to have the pH look low . . . . Just like any other tests that humans design, someone can put their mind to it and get around the test.[63]

Early in the above exchange, it is Farone who is explaining that scientists rely on other researchers, that tests are set up for a reason (e.g., competitive intelligence), that test designs change over time, and that debates surround methodology—and all are represented as benign social aspects of science. At the end of his answers, however, Farone identifies a pejorative feature of the social aspect of science: one can cheat to avoid naturalistic results. Again, we agree with Farone's pragmatic and contextual explanation of social aspects of science as good or bad depending on the circumstances.

The key to discrediting Farone in *Neri* was his inability to produce an example of a testable, alternative cigarette design (supported by consensus among scientists):

Q. Do you have a specific alternative design that you contend R.J. Reynolds should have used that was safer?

A. . . . I've gone through a series of designs for each type of technology . . . . So it's more that one design . . . .

Q. It's not your opinion that the ultimate alternative design is feasible today?

A. Oh, it is . . . . The ultimate alternative design simply carries Premier and Eclipse and Accord to the logical conclusion where you simply deliver a drug, not necessarily nicotine.[64]

Like the disagreement in *Hybritech* over whether Hybritech's technology was obvious—a natural development of existing knowledge—or novel, Farone is claiming that the technology for a safer cigarette already exists, while R.J. Reynolds counsel is claiming that it does not. The "ultimate alternative design," while it may not exist per se, is for Farone present within existing technology and is simply awaiting its logical development.

Q. Would your ultimate alternative design also have nicotine?

A. No, but it depends on what we do about delivering the nicotine. If it's a low level where it shows no effect [on] cardiovascular, it could have.

We right now don't know that such a level exists, but that experimentation could be done . . . .

Q. Is that something that would have to be subject to further research?

A. That's correct . . . .

. . . But one of the things I've been talking to people about is the combination of pyridine and lobeline . . . . [That] would be a logical thing to investigate . . . .

Q. I take it you are not currently prepared to say that the nicotine analog [would be] this combination of pyridine and lobeline?

A. What I'm saying is that these combinations could have been tested. And the fact that they are not tested is an indication that we're not really serious about making safer cigarettes.[65]

Farone begins in a naturalistic framework, claiming that a safer cigarette design exists, but he ends up explaining that it depends on further decisions, experimentation, research, logical steps, and seriousness about finding it. After this shift to a social framework in an attempt to deflect the doubt that the "ultimate alternative design" exists, he returns to a naturalistic framework to claim that a middle-ground, safer cigarette design exists even without the ultimate alternative:

A. I wouldn't wait until . . . I had the perfect nicotine analog . . . . [I]n the meantime, I would reduce the risk . . . .

This is done in stages. We don't shoot the magic bullet [right away]. We can make changes with no further technology . . . .

[W]e're going to use the best filtration mechanisms we know . . . .

Q. [Y]ou don't actually have a set of specifications for this alternative design yet; is that correct . . . ?

A. No . . . when you say specifications, what comes to my mind is a piece of paper that I would give to my people on how to set up the machine that made it and, you know, the chemical purity of the ingredients . . . . Those are very easy.

Once one accepts the premise, it's a simple matter to develop those specifications. So, no, I haven't done that because I don't have a company where I could implement this design. If I did, I would quickly write them down . . . .

Q. Let me ask you this. Reasonable chemists and engineers and cigarette designers can disagree over what the best design is for a cigarette; you would agree with that?

A. That's correct . . . .

Q. Would you agree that there is no consensus in the scientific community as to what constitutes a safer cigarette?

A. I think there's a consensus . . . that not smoking is better. After that, everyone has differing opinions . . . . There's not a consensus on the test.[66]

Faced with a naturalistic argument that specifications for a *somewhat* safer cigarette exist, R.J. Reynolds counsel shifts to a social framework, whereby controversies and a lack of consensus cast doubt on Farone's claims. Safety, of course, is a notoriously social concept—not found in nature—even though Farone tries to frame it as a consensus over naturalistic matters ("not smoking is better"). On the naturalistic side (i.e., the appropriate test), however, consensus is lacking.

The Social and Rhetorical Aspects of Science

The foregoing analysis casts doubt on numerous assumptions concerning expert scientific discourse. First, while the naturalistic or technical framework of expert testimony is often contrasted with both the socially constructed aspect of legal categories and the rhetorical aspect of legal arguments, scientists comfortably move back and forth between naturalistic and social frameworks in their arguments, often for strategic reasons (e.g., to deflect implied criticism). Second, while science can be defined in law as a matter of hypotheses, data, methodology, and consensus, some judges recognize that it is *also* a matter of social contexts, institutionalized credentials, contested representations, consensus-building techniques, rhetorical moves, theoretical commitments, and experimental conventions. Finally, while bias, interest, and motivation are typically framed by lawyers, pejoratively, as barriers to good science, these also characterize the scientific enterprise in its technical success and progress.

In practical terms, therefore, sociotechnical arguments on the part of experts are inevitable, and are not flaws to be remedied. One should not adopt the dichotomy, reflected in idealized views of science, between natural and social, or between technical and nonscientific phenomena—social, historical, rhetorical, and economic structures provide the context for all scientific practice. Reconceiving science as a sociotechnical discourse is not a critique of scientists, but is rather a recognition of science's complexity. Lawyers and judges, of course, readily concede the technical complexity of science, but they should also be interested in the complex oscillation (in scientific discourse) between the social and technical references that anchor scientific arguments. Specifically, rather than assuming that the technical aspects of science are always good and that social determinants—for example, bought-and-paid-for testimony, bias toward a pet theory, or economic motivation—are always bad, lawyers and judges should recognize that recourse to a social framework of explanation *might* signal a lack of technical substance or a rhetorical subterfuge, but it might be an explication of normal, pragmatic science with all of its usual rhetorical, communal, institutional, and economic aspects. The appropriate distinction is therefore not between objective data and human interference, but between strong and weak sociotechnical arguments. When the social framework reflects fraud, lack of data, or sloppy experimental techniques, the technical argument is of course weakened; but when the social framework reflects *funding* that leads to a *negotiated* consensus concerning *acceptable* margins of error in a promising new experimental *convention*, it can add support to a technical argument. Moreover, when a technical argument is destabilized due to genuine disagreements within a particular scientific community, recourse to a social framework is seemingly inevitable, thus the outcome of a scientific dispute may turn on the successful mobilization of social, rhetorical, institutional, historical, and economic entities. Finally, the capacity of judges and juries to evaluate scientific testimony would be enhanced by a pragmatic recognition of the limitations of technical arguments and the often benign, even supportive, role of social frameworks in scientific practice.

ETHNOGRAPHY AND THE IDEALIZED
ACCOUNTS OF SCIENCE IN LAW

> [W]hen sociological observers began to enter the places where scientific knowledge is produced, the laboratory, they found many practices that seemed to share more with daily life outside the lab than with the strict edicts governing knowledge in science, such as universality, objectivity, or reproducibility. Measurement might be based on a very unclear consensus. Techniques might be developed in local settings and depend on local materials and practices . . . . The establishment of findings in the laboratory as facts accepted by the wider scientific community might turn out to be in large part a social process . . . of gaining credibility . . . .[67]

As we have shown in previous chapters, much of the judicial and scholarly literature concerning the so-called *Daubert* four-part test and the new Federal Rule of Evidence 702—namely, that scientific testimony is based on sufficient data and is the product of reliable methods—virtually ignores the social embeddedness of science in favor of a core or bottom-line description of the scientific methodology. Even when decidedly social aspects of the scientific enterprise—for example, funding bias, fraud, or governing research para-digms—are acknowledged, they are seemingly viewed as temporary and ir-relevant to the project of defining "Science."[68] There is little attention paid to the inevitable institutional and rhetorical features of modern science. Our pur-pose in the following section is to explore that failure, explain how some sci-ence studies scholars investigate social embeddedness, and suggest how judges and attorneys might view science differently in light of such studies.

Idealizing Science

> Scientists such as Wolpert . . . happily acknowledge that science is a "social ac-tivity. Every practicing scientist is acutely aware of it. How could one not be?" All he wishes to deny is "that science is merely a social construct with little spe-cial validity."[69]

One of the ways in which science is idealized in judicial and scholarly dis-course is by emphasizing core aspects of science as exclusively significant for admissibility assessments.[70] Core features of science include (i) a scientific hypothesis or theory (or testable theory); (ii) scientific data; (iii) reliable test-ing or methodology, including standards and controls to ensure a low error rate; and (iv) a conclusion, or probable conclusion, with explanatory power. Each of these features of science has an obvious anchor in nature or reality: (i) theories are formulated with reference to perceived reality, (ii) the data is a representation of natural phenomena, (iii) the methodology is how the data is handled, and (iv) a probable conclusion should lead to explanatory power and success. However, each of these core features of science also has an an-chor in social structures, that is, (i) theories reflect personal and communal beliefs and values as to what is important or worth studying, which beliefs and values have a history and refer back to earlier research, institutional train-ing, and professionalization of scientists; (ii) observation of data is mediated by cognitive capacity and theoretical presuppositions (hence the term *theory-laden observation*, which suggests the researcher is looking for some things but not for others); (iii) methodology has a social history of experimental con-ventions, and may vary among fields of research,[71] while measurement tech-nology and inscription devices have a social history related to available re-sources and theoretical paradigms; and (iv) conclusions are made with reference to the scientific community's acceptability standards, arising from the history of science and practical demands.[72] Such social aspects are not, or should not be, particularly controversial, but they are often not identified and discussed as significant in idealized accounts of science. When the U.S. Supreme Court, in *Daubert*, seemed to define science as involving testable theories, a low error rate, peer review and publication, and general acceptance, those elements became topics of discussion in judicial opinions, legal scholarship, and even bar journals and continuing legal education programs. Lawyers and judges, quite naturally, focused their attention on these aspects of science in matters of admissibility of expert testimony.

Significantly, the last two features of the *Daubert* four-part test—peer review/publication and general acceptance—identify social aspects of scientific activity. They are not, however, on the same *level* as testability and low error rate, which are considered to be the markers of valid science.[73] Most of the time, Justice Blackmun opined, valid theories will be the product of the peer review/publication process and will attain general acceptance—while other theories should be viewed with suspicion—but some novel theories will not be peer reviewed or generally accepted.[74] Social aspects of science were thereby downplayed, and an opportunity was missed for a discussion of the institutional and rhetorical characteristics of science that are reflected in the processes of peer review/publication and general acceptance.

Figure 5.1 provides a diagram of how the idealized or core account of science might be presented. This picture of science in law leads judges and lawyers (and therefore juries) to focus solely on adequacy of data and testing, presence of publications, and level of general acceptance in (i) judicial assessments of reliability, (ii) determining appropriate subjects for deposition and cross-examination questions, and (iii) drafting jury instructions.

Even when one who idealizes science acknowledges the social aspects of scientific activity, those aspects can nevertheless be characterized as relatively insignificant or at least as unworthy of serious attention. First, one may distinguish between internal and external factors in scientific activity. Further, one may identify the internal factors as good, that is, as productive and positive, and the external factors as bad, or at least as superfluous to genuine science.[75] Indeed, peer review/publication and general acceptance can be seen as internal to good science; while other internal factors might include institutional gatekeeping (including training and professionalization), methodological preferences, experimental conventions, instrument and measurement technologies, models to represent nature, theoretical paradigms, scientific language, negotiation techniques and strategies for conflict resolution and consensus-building, cognitive capacity and perception, and even values like consistency, honesty, rigor, self-criticism, and reproducibility. Each such factor is a social, not natural, structure, but each can be conceived as conducive to natural scientific inquiry. External factors might include political interests and pressures (including ethical and policy limitations), economic interests, funding bias, fraud, bad or misleading instruments, greed, ambition, rhetoric and persuasion, gender or racial bias, and general cultural values. The problem with the internal/external distinction is that external factors are not al-

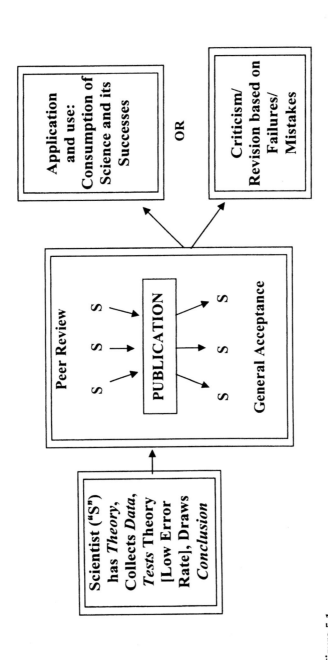

Figure 5.1.

ways bad or superfluous, and internal factors are not always good or productive. Greed, ambition, persuasion, or economic interests might at times produce the best science, while institutional gatekeeping, theoretical paradigms, and models can at times lead scientists astray.

Even though the internal/external distinction breaks down, social factors can also be ignored through a distinction between a context of discovery and a context of justification.[76] The messier aspects of science—for example, greed or ambition—can be categorized as belonging to the context of discovery, where new ideas might come from anywhere,[77] even from sloppy techniques and cultural bias. The validity of science, however, is in this view grounded in the context of justification, which is the idealized picture of science—that is, testability, methodology, reproducibility, and probable conclusions. This distinction, likewise, is problematical because social aspects pervade the context of justification.[78] Finally, another "defense mechanism" against acknowledgement of social aspects is the explanation of error by reference to social influence, and the explanation of success by reference to nature.[79] For example, funding bias or political pressure can be viewed as a mistake that must be eliminated, leaving the impression that social influences can be avoided. All of these characterizations of the social aspects of science—external influences, internal supports, context of discovery, and avoidable errors—function to deflect or to downplay the inevitable institutional and rhetorical character of scientific theory and practice.

Because our narrative above identifies at least twenty social aspects of science in addition to the peer review/publication process, another diagram may be helpful to show how our picture of science can be expanded beyond the previous core (depicted in figure 5.1 as an idealized picture of science). However, the diagram below (see figure 5.2) is also a representation of how most of these social factors can be explained away or rendered superfluous. The external influences depicted above the figure's idealized account of science include examples of the context of discovery (where greed, ambition, or anything such as mistakes or religion might accidentally lead to good, justifiable science), of cultural or social influence, and of erroneous or junk science—all of which may be viewed as eliminable, once identified, by setting a boundary between them and the core activities. Indeed, the core becomes the context of justification, the arena wherein fraud can be caught, mistakes can be corrected, and biased or "interested" science can be falsified. The Internal Supports—the social aspects of science depicted below the core activities on the diagram—are harder to get rid of, but may be dismissed as obvious (i.e., language and perception are givens) and in any event as necessary but benign and unproblematic. If something does go wrong internally—an insufficient

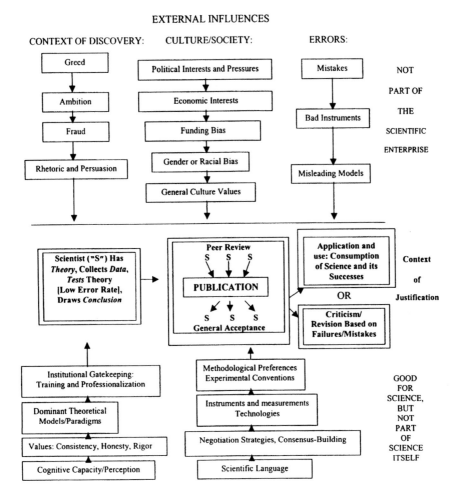

Figure 5.2.

model, a biased laboratory, an inaccurate measurement device—then it becomes an external influence to be moved to the top of the diagram and then eliminated by careful core activities.

The motivation behind such efforts to define science in terms of core, methodological activities is often to distinguish science from nonscience, and to distinguish scientific methodology as a "uniquely rational mode of inference or procedure of inquiry used by all scientists and only by scientists."[80] Doubting that such a method exists, Susan Haack notes that

[s]omething like the "hypothetico-deductive method" . . . really *is* the core of all inquiry, scientific inquiry included; and the fact that scientists, like inquirers of every kind, proceed in this way tells us nothing substantive about whether or when their testing is reliable.[81]

As we noted in the previous chapter, we quite agree that every kind of empirical inquiry, whether by historians, by legal or literary scholars, or by scientists, "involves making an informed guess about the explanation of some event or phenomenon, figuring out the consequences of the explanation's being true, and checking how well those consequences stand up to evidence."[82] We are therefore not interested in strongly distinguishing science from nonscience. However, as an alternative picture of science, and at the risk of appearing to attempt to define science, we include figure 5.3 as a contrast to the idealizations of figure 5.2—note that we have simply rearranged the social aspects of science so that they are *part of* the scientific enterprise. The boundaries between Internal and External and the Not Part of the Scientific Enterprise classification have disappeared to indicate that good science may involve any number of social aspects. We present this diagram as neither normative (as the way science should be done) nor unique to science—one could just as easily substitute a publishing scholar in the humanities for Scientist(s).

In the remainder of this chapter, we want to challenge the dismissive arrangement of influences in figure 5.2 by suggesting that many of these identifiable social aspects of science should remain in play in our legal discourse concerning scientific expertise. This is not to say that every social aspect identified in figure 5.3 is present or significant in every scientific activity, but rather that many social factors are characteristic of science generally, and therefore are as much a part of science as data or an experimental test.

Ethnography and Science

[T]he fact that science is political and deeply embedded in [cultural] events is not simply the now-clichéd, albeit important conclusion of social scientists and historians studying scientists, but is part of the condition of doing science . . . . Some scientists . . . acknowledge their social embeddedness not at all or only in the most indirect and subtle ways; for others it is diversely and strongly expressed.[83]

Ethnomethodology[84] has become an established, if varied, mode of analysis in science studies. In anthropology, "ethnography usually requires learning [another] language, developing key informants, and spending at least one to

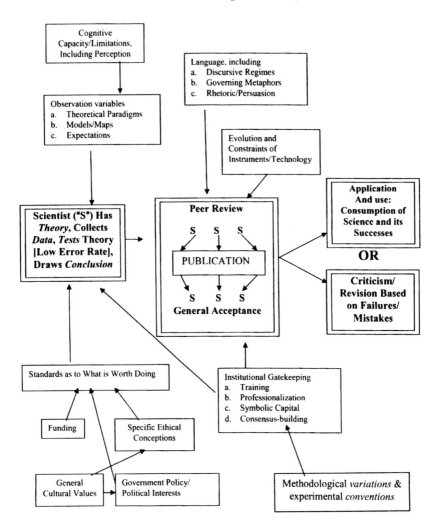

Figure 5.3.

two years of more-or-less continuous participant-observation in a community, organization, or social movement."[85] The method has been borrowed in other disciplines, such as ethnomusicology (wherein the local music of an ethnic community is studied), and in comparative law, for example, by Leonard Pospisil in *The Ethnology of Law* (1978), which focused on the legal system of the Kapauku Papuans of West New Guinea. In science studies, however,

"ethnography" has historically applied loosely to any kind of fieldwork-based method, including short-term observational studies. Thus, in science studies circles the term has a considerably looser usage than in anthropology . . . . For this reason, the term "laboratory studies" is preferable for the first wave of ethnographic studies [which] addressed questions about theoretical issues in the sociology and philosophy of knowledge.[86]

Following scientists through society, or looking over their shoulders, is a means to study the fact-making process, to view "interactions among scientific, governmental, industrial, religious, and other domains of society," and to identify the rituals, values, and material cultures (buildings, machines, equipment) that characterize the scientific enterprise.[87] The anthropological model is justified by viewing science as a subculture with its own languages, conventions, institutional hierarchies, values, and structures for training and professionalization of its members.[88]

Reasons for engaging in ethnographic research, which research usually involves interviewing scientists as *informants* and analyzing the transcripts, vary in science studies.[89] Some scholars want to discern the values at work in science, particularly to reveal unattractive values or to suggest social values to which scientists should be committed.[90] Others want to degrade scientific knowledge, to demonstrate that science is just another cultural activity with no more claim to truth than political theory or religion.[91] Our own sense is that ethnographic research is useful in the effort to understand science or describe "how it really works."[92] Whatever the purpose, the ethnography of science is a growing subdiscipline of science studies that is no longer haphazard or under-theorized. Examples of ethnographic research are published, and materials are available that identify interviewing skills and common blunders,[93] as well as the importance of *indexicality* ("the meaning of a word or utterance is dependant on its context of use"), *reflexivity* ("descriptions are not just *about* something but they are also *doing* something"), and the *documentary method of interpretation* (people understand "events and actions . . . in terms of background expectancies, models, and ideas") in conversation analysis.[94] Because of our concern that idealized accounts of science in law tend toward "stereotypical images of scientists as cut off from society and culture, [and] concerned only with the microworlds of labs and their professional networks," and because of the suggestion in science studies that "the insight concerning the social constructedness and embeddedness of scientific activity . . . is also shared to varying degrees by scientists and scientific institutions themselves,"[95] we decided to interview three neuroscientists concerning their laboratory research. Our goal was to explore, in conversation, some aspects of scientific activity that are not captured in idealizations of science. We chose neuroscientists as informants both because their field is dynamic (and revolutionary within the disciplines of psychiatry and psychology),[96] and because neuroscientists often collapse social existence into natural determinants (hence the term *eliminative materialism*).[97] Our anonymous informants included X, a relatively young but highly credentialed professor; Y, a very successful middle-aged professor (recipient of numerous grants, engaged in commercial consulting, and author of numerous publications and conference papers); and Z, an older, retiring professor at the end of a successful career. Even though we asked similar questions of each—questions concerning each informant's educational background, each informant's current research, and questions directed toward neutrality in science and new ideas in psychology—the particular sociocultural aspects of science discussed by each varied somewhat.

We should emphasize that our informants did not believe that they were engaged professionally in an enterprise that was *primarily* rhetorical, philosophical, or driven by social structures—obviously, they saw their work as grounded in natural phenomena. Each therefore reacted, in different ways, against any suggestion that science is *only* a cultural discourse or belief system. Informant Y was not enamored of the idea that the objects of science are socionatural hybrids, and he was dismissive of philosophy of science in general.[98] Informants X and Z viewed the social aspects of science as *influences*, which could be bad if research was restricted but good if they constituted useful structures in which scientists could work.[99] Nevertheless, in our conversations it was clear that the social aspects of scientific activity were integral to the enterprise of each. Because we were interested in identifying social aspects of science, we began with a catalog—a list or menu derived from the scholarly literature in science studies—of potential social factors. In our interviews, we chose not to inquire about those social factors that most scientists consider anomalous or eliminable, including greed, ambition, fraud, obvious funding bias or corporate agendas, bad measuring instruments, and mistakes or identifiable human error. We also did not focus on cultural variations in scientific research, or public understanding of and influence upon science, each of which has been the subject of critical studies of science.[100] Finally, we tried to distinguish between aspects of science that are, for all practical purposes, inevitable, and those that can be conceived of as problematic or controversial, such as the cultural construction of science in terms of class, race/ethnicity, or gender/sexuality.[101] Focusing on the former, we were left with the following catalog, which is also reflected in figure 5.3:

1. Cognitive capacity/limitations, including perception[102]
2. Standards as to what is interesting or what is worth doing,[103] including:
   a. the effects of funding/patronage
   b. general cultural values (e.g., honesty)
   c. specific ethical conceptions of, for example, unacceptable research

     d. government policy and political interests (which overlap with a, b, and
       c above)
3. Language,[104] including
     a. scientific and discursive regimes
     b. governing metaphors
     c. conventions of rhetoric and persuasion
4. Evolution and constraints of measurement instruments and technology[105]
5. Observation variables,[106] including
     a. dominant theoretical paradigms
     b. models and maps that function as representations of nature
     c. expectations, including their effect on interpretation of data
6. Institutional gatekeeping, including
     a. training
     b. professionalization
     c. symbolic *capital*[107] (social networks, Rolodex cards, positions held,
       previous accomplishments, etc., that lend credibility)
     d. consensus-building and negotiation techniques
7. Methodological *variation* and experimental *conventions*[108]

The above catalog, which was intended to capture ordinary social aspects of science (as opposed to eliminable problems or negative influences), offers both a complex picture of science to supplement idealizations (which emphasize core aspects) *and* a categorization scheme for classifying statements made by the scientists in our interviews. (We did not classify references to core aspects of science, which were numerous, because we take it to be obvious that science involves theories, data collection, and conclusions that promise some level of objectivity, precision, and prediction.) Again, our informants did not address each social category in our conversations; we began each interview with general questions about the informant's background and current research interests, and when we later asked about social aspects of their work, we were intentionally ambiguous. In the following summaries of each interview, therefore, variable responses are to be expected.

Interview with X [A Young Professor]

1. Cognitive capacity/limitations: "I think it's not really practical or even advisable for a single person to try to cover all the bases [in every discipline]."
2. Standards as to what is interesting/important:
     a. Funding: "I think a lot of us whenever we make a pitch to the NIH . . . have to indicate that there is some benefit [that] there is social good

coming out of what we do . . . . When you have a constituency to which you're accountable, you've got to show some meaningful progress. . . . And that is, I think, [an] apparent restriction of thought. . . ."

3. Language: ". . . one of the first things I tell students in a class [is that] because of the nature of the material, . . . they're going to have to learn a lot of vocabulary . . . . It's like learning words in the dictionary [to enhance] the ability to be conversant and to communicate in a succinct and accurate way . . . ."

4. Instruments: [no significant remarks]

5. Observation:
   a. Paradigms: ". . . there's a considerable amount of friction between [those] doing biological psychology, and people at other areas of the [psychology] department. Now the biological psychologists are in literally separated space . . . those are people who have . . . and I'll admit that I'm sort of one of them . . . only a very peripheral interest in the overt behavior of the organisms that they study . . . ."

6. Institutional gatekeeping: Funding requests are forwarded "to a group of peers who are expert, to evaluate your work for several different things. One is scientific novelty. Another one is rigor of the proposal . . . feasibility . . . . And they take into consideration things like your track record; your biographical sketch is an essential component . . . ."

7. Method: [no significant remarks]

Interview with Y: [A Middle-Aged Professor]

1. Cognitive capacity/limitations: ". . . I also recognize the fact that my experience is different from many other humans . . . . Males tend not to think about odors in the same way as females . . . ."

2. Standards as to what is interesting/important:
   a. Funding: ". . . it's important to have an income. In order to have an income you have to stay sort of within the mainstream of science . . . ."

3. Language: "[Our] language is going to change how you think about [mind and body], and this happens in the law when it comes to the insanity defense; our ideas about human behavior are so inherently dualistic . . . . I think changing the way people talk about this and reducing this dualistic language in terms of the descriptions of this physical world will actually be [useful]."

4. Instruments: "It would be absurd to imagine that you didn't have constraints on the outcome you were expecting. By simply choosing a measurement instrument, a device to measure, you are generating hypotheses [that constrain] what's going to happen. We all know that you can measure

one thing and have multiple things happening and then ignore those others . . . ."

5. Observation: "I think one of the more interesting things in science are those people who are at the edge . . . and how they are either embraced or pushed out of regular scientific journals . . . . [Y]ou have a lot of expectations out there . . . . There are an infinite number of solutions so I have to constrain my solutions . . . ."

6. Institutional gatekeeping: "When I asked my advisor if we couldn't do some smell experiments in the lab he said, 'No, we can't, it's just too difficult to control odors and stimulate and so we're not doing that' . . . ."

7. Methodological variation: " . . . we lost evolutionary psychology . . . . It's actually impossible methodologically to compare a goldfish with a dog and people said of course and so it was dropped . . . then suddenly in literally the last five years, you have had this reemergence of people who want to say things about the comparative nature of animals . . . . I think that . . . we're recouching these things, they come and go as fashions, and that's troubling . . . ."

Interview with Z: [An Older Professor]

1. Cognitive capacity/limitations: [no significant remarks]
2. Standards as to what is interesting/important:
   a. Funding: ". . . there were pharmaceutical firms that were very interested especially in following this . . . then [the researchers in England with whom Z was working] approached a couple of big firms that are, I guess, a number of pharmaceutical companies [that] get together and they have a granting agency that . . . support[s] this kind of research . . . the idea was there would be money to last for three years. Well, the money didn't go that far . . . . So they raised [money by going public] . . . ."
   b. Ethical policy constraints: ". . . our new [Bush] administration puts such constraints on using fetal tissue for research . . . . That's an ethical issue that is so important . . . . [Social values are getting in the way of scientific progress] in the [United] States . . . ."
3. Language: [Z agreed that there's an aspect of persuasiveness in science, that is, convincing others that one's work is valuable and deserves funding.]
4. Instruments: [no significant remarks]
5. Observation:
   a. Models: "You can create a stroke in rats by cutting off the carotid arteries and having them on a respirator for about ten minutes, but [you will] lose about 60 percent of the animals, [and] they have the same

> kind of damage you have with a person who's had a heart attack . . . .
> So [some] think if they could directly damage those cells and not lose
> so many animals . . . that would be a good kind of animal model . . . ."

6. Institutional gatekeeping: "So we did one study that for the longest [time just] sat there and nobody paid any attention to it, and just within the last two or three years, people really started paying attention . . . ."

7. Methodology: [no significant remarks]

The value of ethnography, or conversation analysis, is its informality—it is part anthropological interview with a key informant and part journalistic profile, thus the setting allows for unanticipated turns and linkages in a way that questionnaires sent to scientists might not.[109]

For example, a scientist is not likely to emphasize, in a formal paper at a scientific meeting, general reflections on scientific practice; such reflections would be more common at a philosophy conference, but the speaker would not likely be a scientist! In the interview with young Professor X, we were pleasantly surprised—given the thesis of this book—that he spoke so comfortably about the limitations of his disciplinary perspective, the need to satisfy a funding constituency, the unique languages of science, and the importance of credentials. Likewise, middle-aged Professor Y, even though he initially scoffed at philosophical and social studies of science, carefully explained the significance of an investigator's gender, the impact of language on thought, the constraints of expectations on the part of the investigator *and* the scientific establishment, and the historical evolution of scientific theories. Perhaps it would be expected that older Professor Z, at the end of his career, would be reflective on the nature of science, but he was more anxious to talk about his ongoing research, the success of which was determined by funding mechanisms, political and ethical restraints, and a growing communal recognition that his collaborative work was important. In short, these interviews confirmed our hunch that science is far more pragmatic and contextual than is suggested by reductionistic core or methodological pictures of scientific activity.

Scientists' own formal accounts of their work are not likely to emphasize the institutional and rhetorical aspects of that work, except in the case of autobiographies. However, in the relatively unstructured context of a few ethnographic interviews, where the formalities of "quantification and statistical analysis [play] a subordinate role at most," a scientist's verbal descriptions and explanations reveal a great deal about the social, rhetorical, and institutional aspects of science.[110] Of course, ethnography is obviously a supplement to, and not a replacement of, the sociology of science generally (which establishes the theory that science is a social activity), the philosophy of science, and the history of science, each of which includes critical scholars who offer insights as to how science *really* works in contrast to popular or idealized accounts of scientific progress, including idealized accounts within each discipline.

Courtroom Scientific Expertise and the Social Aspects of Science

> Of course social factors influence the course of science. The only controversy concerns which social factors are operative in which situations and how powerful those social factors turn out to be.[111]

While bias on the part of an expert is often viewed as anathema to good science, one might also view disciplinary, institutional, occupational, or methodological bias as part and parcel of science. As to the former characterization (bias is bad), consider F. Lee Bailey and Henry Rothblatt's *Cross-Examination in Criminal Trials* (1978):

> The good forensic pathologist is detached and objective. However, you will encounter some pathologists who will not be quite so professional . . . . You must be aware of the signs indicating that a medical examiner is biased . . . .[112]

Contrast that warning with Dr. Bernard Diamond's view that "all witnesses, regardless of who engaged them, identify closely with their own opinions and unintentionally introduce as a result a certain degree of bias and deviation from their oath to tell the truth . . . ." Experts are "bound to be biased and partial and strongly motivated toward advocacy of [a] particular prejudiced point of view."[113] Such inevitable bias in science is more readily acknowledged concerning *social* scientists as "human beings with social identities, beliefs, and values that link them to some causes and parties more than to others."[114] However, the notion that social science "depends upon, benefits from, and is interdependent with extra-scientific institutions" and that "financial allocations have overt or covert strings attached [that] shape what gets studied [and] perhaps what is concluded"[115] is arguably applicable to the hard sciences. For example,

> it is not possible to pursue either a programme of research or a career in [complex areas of medicine] in isolation from a limited set of key institutions; and the high financial costs of maintaining these institutions have led researchers towards an increasingly close relationship with those industries that have a direct interest in the extent and content of knowledge about particular kinds of ill health.[116]

Nevertheless, such social analyses of expertise are rare in judicial opinions, scholarly legal commentary, or treatises on cross-examination of expert witnesses. Interestingly, there *is* a contemporary discourse, in various publications and on websites, concerning the potential bias of science toward large corporate defendants—for example, pharmaceutical companies—that support research and thereby are seen to control scientific knowledge. While such criticism is admirable for its recognition of the social, institutional, and rhetorical aspects of science, it often proceeds on the basis of an idealized view of science, and as if the best science is not also social, institutional, and rhetorical.

Roger Smith and Brian Wynne have attempted to explain the lack of attention to contextual—evoking disciplinary perspectives, institutional or occupational affiliations, and methodological commitments—models of scientific disputes in law. They identify a persistent

> hope that the objectivity of science will provide a firm and authoritative input, giving decisions a factual basis that cannot be questioned. That the science often appears equivocal is put down to procedural problems rather than inherent properties of scientific knowledge or methods . . . .[117]

Insights from the sociology of scientific knowledge, for example, "that even the most disciplined and objective observation is never free of theoretical and thus interpretive precommitments," or that a "proven fact is ultimately a social achievement among scientists,"[118] do not pass easily into law as general propositions.

In the next chapter, we conclude our study by discussing the challenges and opportunities offered by the appropriation of science studies into law, not only in the context of litigation but more broadly in the policy arena.

NOTES

1. Alberto Cambrosio, Peter Keating, and Michael Mackenzie, "Scientific Practice in the Courtroom: Construction of Sociotechnical Identities in a Biotechnology Patent Dispute," 37 *Soc. Prob.* 275, 291 (1990).

2. *See id.*, discussing *Hybritech Inc. v. Monoclonal Antibodies, Inc.*, 623 F. Supp. 1344 (N.D. Cal. 1985) and 802 F.2d 1367 (9th Cir. 1986).

3. *See id.* at 275.

4. *See id.* at 277.

5. *See* J. S. Oteri, M. G. Weinberg, and M. S. Pinales, "Cross-Examination of Chemists in Drug Cases," in *Science in Context: Readings in the Sociology of Science* (ed. Barry Barnes and David Edge, 1982) at 250–59 (detailing how to attack chemists in drug cases for their lack of education and qualifications, carelessness in the laboratory, financial bias, and failure to perform adequate tests); James M. Shellow, "The

Limits of Cross-Examination," 34 *Seton Hall L. Rev.* 317 (2003) (using examples from cross-examinations over many years, the author variously illustrates a refusal to recognize authoritative scientific writings or to review relevant research, a failure to understand basic scientific principles, a refusal to produce underlying data, a refusal to compare data with published data or other test data on the same sample, a failure to perform accepted tests, a failure to review prior errors, a reliance on subjective methodology, and a refusal to admit error rate).

6. Cambrosio et al., *supra* note 1, at 276–77, discussing 623 F. Supp. 1344 (N.D. Cal. 1985) and 802 F.2d 1367 (9th Cir. 1986).

7. *See id.* at 277.

8. *See* Cambrosio et al., *supra* note 1, at 279.

9. *See id.; see also* 623 F. Supp. at 1346, quoted with approval in 802 F.2d at 1375.

10. Cambrosio et al., *supra* note 1, at 277.

11. *See id.* at 277:

> For instance, the content of categories such as "fundamental research" and "industry" can be explained by showing how witnesses, in the course of expert testimony, construct different distributions of the research and development continuum, and how they relate technical statements and devices to "social [sub]groups" which then become criteria of identity.

12. *See* Cambrosio et al., *supra* note 1, at 279, quoting Herzenberg in the *Hybritech* trial transcript, vol. 11, p. 1333.

13. *See id.*, citing the *Hybritech* trial transcript, vol. 11, pp. 1405–6.

14. *See* Cambrosio et al., *supra* note 1, at 280.

15. *See id.*

16. *See* Cambrosio et al., *supra* note 1, at 281. The defendant's "lawyer's counter-strategy was to deny the context and cling to 'universal' definitions, such as those contained in a dictionary . . . ." *See id.*

17. *See id.*

18. *See id.*, quoting from the *Hybritech* trial transcript, vol. 1, pp. 73–75 (emphasis added by authors).

19. *See* Cambrosio et al., *supra* note 1, at 282, quoting from the *Hybritech* trial transcript, vol. 5, p. 406.

20. *See* Cambrosio et al., *supra* note 1, at 282–83.

21. *Id.*

22. *See id.* at 284, quoting Gary David (without citation).

23. *See id.*, quoting Gary David in the *Hybritech* trial transcript, vol. 14, p. 1885.

24. *See* Cambrosio et al., *supra* note 1, at 284, citing to Nisonoff in the *Hybritech* trial transcript, vol. 12, p. 1525.

25. *See* Cambrosio et al., *supra* note 1, at 284.

26. *See id.* at 285.

27. *See id.* at 284–85.

28. *See id.* at 290.

29. *Id.*

30. *See* 802 F.2d at 1375.

31. *See* 623 F. Supp. 1344, 1350–51, and 1355.

32. *See* 802 F.2d at 1372–74.

33. 243 F. Supp. 2d 508 (D. S.C. 2001). The motion was also granted because the defendant was not liable (i) under state unfair trade practices laws, (ii) for negligent misrepresentation, or (iii) for civil conspiracy.

34. *See* 243 F. Supp. 2d at 519, citing *Daubert v. Merrell Dow Pharmaceuticals*, 509 U.S. 579 (1993).

35. *See* Deposition of William A. Farone, PhD, [July 20, 2000, Irvine, CA], *Labelle v. Philip Morris, Inc.*, U.S. Dist. Court, South Carolina—Charleston Division, Civ. Action No. 2:98-32 35-23, at 7–8.

36. *See id.* at 21–22.

37. *See id.* at 32.

38. *See id.* at 70–71, referring to Farone's publication titled "Recent Trends in Cigarette Industry Science."

39. *See id.* at 72–74.

40. *See id.* at 40.

41. *See id.* at 76–77.

42. *See id.* at 79–80.

43. *See* Farone deposition, *supra* note 35, at 80–81.

44. *See id.* at 81–84.

45. *See id.* at 84.

46. *See id.* at 102.

47. *See id.* at 103–6.

48. *See id.* at 116.

49. *See id.* at 117.

50. *See id.* at 118.

51. *See id.* at 119.

52. *See id.*

53. *See id.* at 121–23.

54. *See id.* at 124.

55. *See id.* at 125.

56. *See id.* at 134–35.

57. *See id.* at 191.

58. *See id.* at 208–9, 212. "So I'm not quarreling with their result. I'm just saying that the product we had identified for sale was not to put this into a plug space plug on the end of every cigarette." *Id.* at 213.

59. *See id.* at 226.

60. *See* 2000 WL 33911224 (N.D.N.Y.) [not reported F. Supp. 2d], at *14 ("Dr. Farone's testimony does not satisfy the reliability test of *Daubert*").

61. *See* Deposition of William Anthony Farone, PhD [Sept. 22, 1999], *Neri v. R.J. Reynolds Tobacco Co.*, at 25, 76–77.

62. *See id.* at 100–101, 109.

63. *See id.* at 111–18.

64. *See id.* at 150–51.

65. *See id.* at 152–56.

66. *See id.* at 156–57, 169–70, 254–55, 308–9.

67. Emily Martin, *Flexible Bodies: Tracking Immunity in American Culture—from the Days of Polio to the Age of Aids* 6 (1994).

68. *See, e.g.*, Erica Beecher-Monas, "The Heuristics of Intellectual Due Process: A Primer for Triers of Science," 75 *N.Y.U. L. Rev.* 1563 (2000). Beecher-Monas begins her "primer" with a strong acknowledgment of science as culture-bound, *id.* at 1576, but then the elements of her "heuristic" are reduced to hypothesis, data, inferences, methodology, and probable conclusion, *id.* at 1589–90.

69. David Hull, "The Professionalization of Science Studies: Cutting Some Slack," 15 *Biol. and Phil.* 61, 85 (2000), quoting Lewis Wolpert, "Response to Fuller," 24 *Soc. Stud. Sci.* 745, 745 (1994).

70. *See, e.g.*, Beecher-Monas, *supra* note 68; *see also* the scholarship discussed in David S. Caudill and Richard E. Redding, "Junk Philosophy of Science? The Paradox of Expertise and Interdisciplinarity in Federal Courts," 57 *Wash. and Lee L. Rev.* 685, 741–43 (2000).

71. *See* David Goodstein, "How Science Works," in *Reference Manual on Scientific Evidence* (2d ed. 2000), at 70: "At the most fundamental level, it is impossible to observe nature without having some reason to choose what is worth observing and what is not worth observing"; "Popper believed all science begins with a prejudice, or perhaps more politely, a theory or hypothesis"; "we don't really know what the scientific method is"; *see also* Gary Edmond, "Judicial Representations of Scientific Evidence," 63 *Mod. L. Rev.* 216, 220 (2000) ("There is no universal scientific method determining every aspect of scientific practice").

72. *See* Philip Kitcher, "A Plea for Science Studies," in *A House Built on Sand: Exposing Postmodernist Myths About Science* (ed. Noretta Koertge, 1998), at 37 ("the practical demands and the history of research standards also help determine what will count as acceptable solutions, specifying, for example, the precision that an answer must achieve if it is to be applicable").

73. Testability and low error rate were identified, without qualification, as features of science, while peer review/publication and general acceptance were factors that may not always be present. *Daubert*, 509 U.S. at 593–94.

74. 509 U.S. at 593–94.

75. *See* Sandra Harding, *Is Science Multicultural? Postcolonialisms, Feminisms, and Epistemologies* 2–3 (1998):

> A central assumption of [the conventional] theory of scientific knowledge is that the success of modern science is insured by its internal features—experimental method or scientific method more generally, science's standards for maximizing objectivity and rationality, the use of mathematics to express nature's laws . . . .
>
> Therefore, when sciences function at their very best, their institutions, cultures, and practices . . . should be understood to provide the necessary conditions for sciences to do their work, but they should not influence the results of research in any culturally distinctive way. Any and all social values and interests that might initially get into the results of scientific research should be firmly weeded out as soon as possible through subsequent critical vigilance.

76. *See* Michael M. J. Fischer, "Eye(I)ing the Sciences and Their Signifiers (Language, Tropes, Autobiographers): InterViewing for a Cultural Studies of Science and Technology," in *TechnoScientific Imaginaries: Conversations, Profiles, and Memoirs* (ed. George E. Marcus, 1995) at 63–64:

> Scientists distinguish between discovery (which may be serendipitous) and confirmation/falsification, between the sociology of science and the content of science . . . . [Such] accounts . . . ignore or downplay the sociological and political environments that enable them.

77. *See* Goodstein, *supra* note 77, at 70 ("Nobody can say where the theory comes from"). *See also* Ian Hacking, "How Inevitable Are the Results of Successful Science?" in *Proceedings of the 1998 Biennial Meeting of the Philosophy of Science Association, Part II, Symposia Papers*, 67 *Phil. Sci.* S 58, S 69 (Supplement) (2000):

> [I]t is patently obvious that which questions get asked, taken seriously, investigated, funded, reported, analyzed, and so forth is the result of social processes, human interactions, and current interests. Very few detailed questions are asked about the most widespread tropical diseases because there is no money in it for drug companies . . . .

78. *See* Werner Callebaut, *Taking the Naturalist Turn, or, How Real Philosophy of Science is Done* 210–14 (conversations with William Bechtel, Thomas Nickles, and other philosophers of science):

> Bechtel: . . . Examining the work of scientists, . . . I came to realize what proportion of their time was devoted to social activities and how important those were in determining the intellectual content of their work. Such things as which scientist would respond to which other and what experiment someone would do were affected . . . . Even [conforming to a prescribed style in a scientific text] is an important social constraint: you realize that scientists are writing in a particular way because that's the only style that's acceptable to get their ideas across. They're fitting into a channel . . . . Also, I came to realize that there is a dynamic that involves who else is in the community and that this influences how one scientist uses words to establish something . . . .

> Callebaut: Back to justification. You [Nickles] make a daring claim . . . that in a sense all justification—and hence all rationality—is at bottom social [*citing inter alia* Thomas Nickles, "Lakatosian Heuristics and Epistemic Support," 38 *Brit. J. Phil. Sci.* 181–205 (1987)].

> Nickles: It sounds daring, but in a way it's trivial. At bottom what else is there? Justification comes down to addressing human critics . . . . [It] is ultimately a matter of *what the critical community lets you get away with* . . . . The important philosophical implication is that justification as it really operates in ongoing inquiry is quite *local*. The arguments and moves that make a difference, that *cause* investigators to behave one way rather than another, are typically quite local.

See also Steven Shapin, *The Scientific Revolution* 10 (1996) ("There is as much society inside the scientist's laboratory, and internal to the development of scientific knowledge, as there is outside").

79. *See* Jonathan Potter, *Representing Reality: Discourse, Rhetoric and Social Construction* 19 (1996):

> False belief could be directly explained through a "social fact" (personality, prejudice and so on) disrupting the proper operation of scientific norms. True belief . . . arises directly from a careful investigation of how the world is. Put simply, in this view of science, the facts themselves determine truth, while error is explained by processes of a psychological or social nature. The consequence of this is that with true belief there was nothing to explain save for how the conditions for proper scientific inquiry came about and how those conditions are undermined.
>
> . . . In effect, . . . the [sociology of error] tradition . . . bracketed off the study of facts themselves and contented itself with examining their sociological context. A full sociological analysis of the *content* of science—of scientific ideas, theories, methods and so on—was reserved only for falsehoods.

80. *See* Susan Haack, "Disentangling *Daubert*: An Epistemological Study in Theory and Practice," 5 J. *Phil., Sci and L.* 4 [online at www.psljournal.com/archives/all/haackpaper.cfm].

81. *See id.*

82. *See id.*

83. George Marcus, "Introduction," in *TechnoScientific Imaginaries*, *supra* note 76, at 7.

84. *See* Michael Moerman, *Talking Culture: Ethnography and Conversation Analysis* ix (1988), *quoting* Harold Garfinkel, *Studies in Ethnomethodology* vii–viii (1967):

> The term "ethnomethodology" . . . is the proper name for viewing "the objective reality of social facts as an ongoing accomplishment of the concerted activities of daily life," and for "discovering the formal properties of common-place . . . actions 'from within' actual settings, as ongoing accomplishments of those settings."

Moerman distinguishes "conversation analysis"—the study of "the organization of everyday talk"—from ethnography, that is, "understanding how people make sense of their lives," but says that conversation analysis is within the intellectual tradition of ethnomethodology and must be coupled with ethnography. Moerman, *supra*, at ix–x.

85. David Hess, *Science Studies: An Advanced Introduction* 134 (1997).

86. *Id.*

87. *See id.* at 135.

88. *See* Bruno Latour, *We Have Never Been Modern* 102 (1993) (citations omitted):

> [The ethnographer] sets out to analyze one tribe . . . for example, scientific researchers or engineers . . . . Her tribe of scientists claims that in the end they are completely separating their knowledge of the world from the necessities of politics and morality. In the observer's eyes, however, this separation is never very visible . . . . [The ethnographer's] informers claim that they have access to Nature, but the ethnographer sees perfectly well that they have access only to a vision, a representation of Nature that she herself cannot distinguish neatly from politics and social interests.

89. *See generally* Marcus, *supra* note 83, and the ethnographic conversations and commentaries collected in *TechnoScientific Imaginaries, supra* note 76.

90. *See, e.g.*, Langdon Winner, "Social Constructivism: Opening the Black Box and Finding it Empty," 16 *Science as Culture* 427 (1993) (arguing that social studies of science and technology should not be neutral reports but morally and politically evaluative).

91. Jonathan Potter, for example, describes the social constructivist

argument . . . that there is nothing epistemologically special about scientific work. Scientific knowledge production does not have principled differences from knowledge in legal or everyday settings.

Potter, *supra* note 79, at 35. Ethnomethodology or conversation analysis offers critics of science a tool for studying "the methods people use for producing and understanding factual descriptions." *Id.* at 42.

92. *See* Marcus, *supra* note 83, at 7:

[B]eginning to ask how scientists have faith in their own activity, or in what ways their perceptions of what they are doing are changing, given some form of distinctive consciousness about the social and cultural construction of their activity, generates a completely transformed and vast field of inquiry on which a distinctly *cultural* studies of science might establish itself. The reflexivity brings a range of new factors *explicitly* into the production of science, and in this sense, makes it more directly cultural, or blended with concerns that were thought to be external to scientific activity.

93. *See, e.g.*, Charles L. Briggs, *Learning How to Ask: A Sociolinguistic Appraisal of the Role of the Interview in Social Science Research* (1986).

94. *See* Potter, *supra* note 79, at 43, 47, and 49. A useful example of indexicality and problems of interpretation appears in Michael Moerman and Harvey Sacks, "On 'Understanding' in the Analysis of Natural Conversation," in Moerman, *supra* note 84, at appendix B:

Roger says: "Ken, face it, you're a poor little rich kid." Ken then says: "Yes, Mommy. Thank you." Roger then says: "Face the music." We are sure that you, like those present, [understood] Ken's "Mommy" as a deliberate and consequential misidentification of Roger, and not as an error, or as a correct identification of someone not present—Ken's mother.

95. *See* Marcus, *supra* note 83, at 7.

96. *See* Joseph Dumit, "Twenty-first Century PET: Looking for Mind and Morality through the Eye of Technology," in *TechnoScientific Imaginaries, supra* note 76, at 114–16 (ethnographic analysis of scientists working in PET [positron emission tomography]):

Dumit: Nancy Andreason, she has written about the biological evolution in psychiatry. You were in medical school during this time. Did you also get the other side of psychiatry?

[Joseph] Wu: Oh, very much so. I would say that most of the psychiatrists in this [University of California, Irvine] department are still analytically, dynamically focused. I would say that biologically oriented psychiatrists still make up a minority of the faculty, maybe thirty to forty percent.

97. *See id.* at 113:

Dumit: This [Washington University] is one of the centers of biological psychology.

[Michel] Ter-Pogossian: Yes, indeed, there are few followers of Freud . . . . But I don't know what the human mind is. Don't misunderstand me, I'm not being difficult about that. But it is probably related to the brain. If you remove the brain, there is not much mind left.

Dumit: Right. I haven't met anybody involved with PET who is not at least that, the eliminative materialist, as it's called.

Ter-Pogossian: Is that what it is?

Dumit: Without the brain, you are nothing. At least that much is material.

Ter-Pogossian: Beyond that, it really starts getting difficult . . . .

98. *See* David S. Caudill, Interview with Y (unpublished transcript), at 7–8:

Caudill: [A] lot of ethnographic scholars in science studies are saying that what they're finding is a breakdown in any sort of Cartesian separation between subject and object . . . . Also, your comments about every time you're dealing with an object in the lab, the brain activity regarding smell, that's not different from a person deciding to sit in a different place in the bus [in which an odor was placed in one seat]; . . . was that a social activity, not sitting [in a particular seat] on the bus, or was that a natural object . . . in the brain? The answer is it's both and neither, it is a quasi-object, it's something between the two . . . .

Y: . . . I just cannot believe that . . . . I find I'm reminded, my old advisor who said that he really liked philosophy until he reached adolescence and then he went on to other pursuits. I can't believe that is a viable argument and it seems to me specious . . . . What other world is there besides the natural world?

99. *See* David S. Caudill, Interview with Z (unpublished transcript), at 15–16:

Caudill: [S]ome scholars say that science is never neutral, it's not in isolation, but there's always particular institutional settings, that there's always value choices as to what's important, there's always commitments as to what you're looking for because your discipline has a history and it's pulling for certain things . . . .

Z: You know it seems like to a certain extent you almost have to have that kind of structure . . . . But the problem is of course if you have too much structure you really scare people off or else you really kind of prevent them developing the potential that they have.

See also David S. Caudill, Interview with X (unpublished transcript), at 12–14:

Caudill: [S]cience studies scholars suggest that science is never neutral, it always involves particular institutional settings with their own language and standards of persuasion, it's always got value choices as to what's important . . . .

X: Well, I think it's a double-edged sword . . . . Yes, science is not neutral . . . there's nobody handing out lots of money to just let us go free in the laboratory . . . . I know that
that was practically the environment . . . in the late 60's to the early 70's . . . . I think that
was extremely good for science. And I think it was bad because it created this public perception . . . why was the taxpayer paying for *that*? . . . On the other hand, I think that it really causes scientists to think long and hard about what it is they plan to do.

100. Regarding cultural variations, *see* Sharon Traweek, *Beamtimes and Lifetimes*
(1988) (comparing Japanese and Western physicists, exploring roles of national and
gender cultures in the shaping of scientific institutions and practices); *see* Hess, *supra*
note 85, at 134–35 ("Sharon Traweek's ethnographic studies of physicists, based on
over a decade of ethnographic fieldwork, are often regarded as a landmark for the beginning of the second wave of ethnography [the first wave was produced by Europeans trained in sociology and philosophy]." Regarding public influence on science,
see Steven Epstein, *Impure Science: Aids, Activism, and the Politics of Knowledge*
(1996) (demonstrating the impact of AIDS activists on medical research and funding).

101. *See generally* David Hess, *Science and Technology in a Multicultural World:
The Cultural Politics of Facts and Artifacts* (1995); *see also* Harding, *supra* note 75.

102. *See* Ronald N. Giere, *Science Without Laws* 48–53 (1999) (discussing "the biological and psychological mechanisms underlying the cognitive capacities of individual
scientists," *id.* at 49, and the need to look to cognitive science to explore those mechanisms); *see also* Nancy J. Nersessian, "Opening the Black Box: Cognitive Science and
the History of Science," 10 *Osiris* 194–211 (1995) (discussing cognitive history of science, cognitive science, and the investigation of creativity, conceptual innovations, technological innovations, communicative practices, and the role of training in science).

103. *See* Kitcher, *supra* note 72, at 4 ("The social structures in which science is
embedded affect the kinds of questions that are taken to be most significant and,
sometimes, the answers that are proposed and accepted").

[T]he kinds of problems singled out as important depend in part on the history of the field
and on the wider interests of members of society . . . . [S]ome problems are especially significant . . . partly because of the history of research [in the field], partly because of what
it is . . . possible to do, and partly because of the practical consequences of certain forms
of inquiry when applied to the problems of certain kinds of societies.

Id. at 37.
See also Pierre Bourdieu, "The Specificity of the Scientific Field and the Social Conditions of the Progress of Reason," in *The Science Studies Reader* (ed. Mario Biagi-
oli, 1999), at 32–33, quoting Fred Reif, *The Competitive World of the Pure Scientist*,
134 *Science* 1957–62 (1961):

[I]t is pointless to distinguish between strictly scientific determinations and strictly social determinations of practices that are essentially overdetermined . . . . Fred Reif shows . . . how
artificial and indeed impossible it is to distinguish between intrinsic and extrinsic interest . . . :
"A scientist strives to do research which he considers important. But intrinsic satisfaction and
interest are not his only reasons . . . . The scientist wants his work to be not only interesting
to himself but also important to others." What is regarded as important and interesting is what
is likely to be recognized by others as important and interesting . . . .

104. *See* Timothy Lenoir, "Inscription Practices and Materialities of Communication," in *Inscribing Science: Scientific Texts and the Materiality of Communication* (ed. Timothy Lenoir, 1998), at 1–19.

> Considerations about language, whether Kuhn-inspired in quantitative linkages between scientific publications or concerns about Wittgensteinian language games and forms of life, have always been part of science studies in one form or another . . . .
> [S]cholars from the side of literature studies have begun to focus on the role of rhetorical practice and techniques of persuasion in scientific texts, on narrative structures and metaphor in the internal structure of scientific work, and on the semiosis among scientific narratives and grand cultural narratives, represented in literature, museum exhibits, and popular culture, as means for the construction and stabilization of scientific artifacts.

Id. at 1, 3. *See also* Joseph Rouse, *Engaging Science: How to Understand its Practices Philosophically* 158–65 (1996) (discussing the turn to narrative in science studies).

105. *See* Hess, *supra* note 101, at 3: "Even apparently transparent observations, such as machine inscriptions of data, are social because machine design is the product of a history that involves social negotiation, as are decisions over calibration and how to interpret machine inscriptions."

106. *See id.* at 3:

> What people expect to observe, are able to observe, and want to observe are all shaped in part by their theories and assumptions, which in turn are outcomes of discussions and controversies in which social negotiation is critical . . . . (However, . . . this claim does not mean that observations have nothing to do with reality: observations are simultaneously socially shaped and representative of a "real" material or social world.)

See also Donna J. Haraway, "Situated Knowledges: The Science Question in Feminism and the Privilege of Partial Perspective," in *The Science Studies Reader, supra* note 103, at 177:

> [A]ll eyes, including our own organic ones, are active perceptual systems, building in translations and specific *ways* of seeing . . . . There is no unmediated photograph or passive camera obscura in scientific accounts of bodies and machines; there are only highly specific visual possibilities, each with a wonderfully detailed, active, partial way of organizing worlds.

107. *See* Hess, *supra* note 101, at 118:

> Some researchers have found Bourdieu's [concept] of symbolic capital . . . to be particularly useful. One might think of symbolic capital as status viewed through a political economy lens. Symbolic capital can be saved and spent, hoarded and wasted, accumulated and invested, and transformed into financial capital. In terms of science, symbolic capital might be operationalized as a scientist's CV and Rolodex, that is a set of career achievements and a network . . . similar to the concepts of reputation and recognition in the sociology of science.

See also Bourdieu, *supra* note 103, at 33.

108. *See* Hess, *supra* note 101, at 3:

> Decisions on appropriate methods, criteria for establishing replication, statistical measures, quantitative versus qualitative measurement, and so on are shaped by rhetoric, network politics, disciplinary cultures, gender socialization patterns, and so on. There is no single Scientific Method to which all scientists can refer; instead, laboratory procedures are opportunistic and contingent on social factors.

109. *See* Roger Smith and Brian Wynne, "Introduction," in *Expert Evidence: Interpreting Science in the Law* (ed. R. Smith and B. Wynne, 1989), at 11:

> We all benefited from extensive discussions with practitioners in the science-law area. Many of these discussions took the form of a relatively unstructured interview . . . . From the viewpoint of the empirical Social Sciences, our method is too informal to count as "method," but, given a deliberate orientation towards qualitative issues, it has served its purpose.

110. *See* Paul Atkinson and Martyn Hammersly, "Ethnography and Participant Observation," in *Strategies of Qualitative Inquiry* (ed. Norman K. Denzin and Yvonna S. Lincoln, 1998), at 111.

111. *See* Hull, *supra* note 69, at 74.

112. F. Lee Bailey and Henry B. Rothblatt, *Cross-Examination in Criminal Trials* 241 (1978).

113. Bernard L. Diamond, "The Fallacy of the Impartial Expert," in *Readings in Law and Psychiatry* (eds. Richard C. Allen, Elyce Zenoff Ferstor, and Jesse G. Rubin, 1975), at 219, 221.

114. *See* Mark A. Chesler, Joseph Sanders, and Debra S. Kalmuss, *Social Science in Court: Mobilizing Experts in the School Desegregation Cases* 63 (1988).

115. *See id.* at 63–64.

116. Jeremy Green, "Industrial Ill Health, Expertise, and the Law," in *Expert Evidence, supra* note 109, at 118–20.

117. *See* Smith and Wynne, *supra* note 109, at 1. Our phrase "disciplinary perspectives, institutional or occupational affiliations, and methodological commitments" is a paraphrase of Green's category of "contextual explanations" of scientific disputes. *See* Green, *supra* note 116, at 118–20.

118. *See* Brian Wynne, "Establishing the Rules of Laws: Constructing Expert Authority," in *Expert Evidence, supra* note 109, at 23, 28.

Chapter Six

Science Studies for Law

SCIENCE AS A FOREIGN CULTURE

[These laboratory scientists] appear to have developed considerable skills in setting up devices which can pin down elusive figures, traces, or inscriptions in their craftwork, and in the art of persuasion. The latter skill enables them to convince others that what they do is important, that what they say is true. . . . They are so skillful, indeed, that they manage to convince others that they are not being convinced but that they are simply following a consistent line of interpretations of available evidence. . . . Not surprisingly, our anthropological observer experienced some dis-ease in handling such a tribe. Whereas other tribes believe in gods or complicated mythologies, the members of this tribe insist that their activity is in no way to be associated with beliefs, a culture, or a mythology.[1]

In this excerpt, one can observe the appropriation from anthropology of ethnographic methodology by scholars who work in science studies. In anthropology, the paradigm example of ethnography is the participant-observer of an exotic tribe or traditional culture, but the "application of ethnographic method by Western anthropologists and sociologists to the investigation of their own societies has been a central feature of twentieth-century social science."[2] In science studies, the "tribe of scientists" has become the object of laboratory studies, exemplified by Bruno Latour's two-year study at the Salk Institute of Biological Studies in La Jolla, California.[3] Just as the goal of traditional ethnography was to understand a foreign culture—by learning its language, developing key informants, and so forth—the goal of ethnographic studies of scientific practices is to understand how science works. One might ask, however, whether and how these studies are useful to the law.

Understanding science is also an ongoing project in the law, since "science has become, and will forever more be, a tool upon which the law must sometimes rely . . . ."[4] While judges and lawyers "are not known for their expertise in science," new standards of scientific validity in the *Daubert* Trilogy and in the Federal Rules of Evidence require that federal trial judges (and many state judges) act as gatekeepers, and that lawyers meet the standard of scientific validity when offering scientific expertise. Viewed optimistically, "there are signs that a 'third culture' is emerging in the law. This third culture would be one that integrates a sophisticated understanding of science into legal decisionmaking."[5] In any event, the need for judges and lawyers to understand science is clear, which suggests that an interdisciplinary engagement with the field of science studies would be beneficial to law. Dissimilarities, however, between science studies and the project of developing sophisticated law and science relations, are immediately apparent.

We have argued that the views of many trial judges and scholars can be characterized by a certain idealization of, and dependence upon, science as a determinative source of stable knowledge for law. This is neither to say that they revere all science and all scientific experts—there's junk science, and experts can be discredited—nor that they believe that science deals in timeless certainties. But they are not critical of valid science and credible experts. In other words, they have adopted science's self-image, such that their legal *accounts* of the scientific enterprise generally mirror the internal accounts of scientists themselves.[6] In science studies, however, the very product of the discipline has been an alternate account of the scientific enterprise that challenges both internal accounts and popular idealizations. For example, while an internal or idealized account of the success of a new scientific theory may refer to a hypothesis that was confirmed by data collection, an alternative account may explain the theory's success in terms of social circumstances, institutional authority, and rhetorical networks.[7] This can be, and has been, viewed as a critique of science itself,[8] though most proponents of such alternative accounts view their work as primarily descriptive *and* as critical only of idealized "accounting practices."[9] Far from trying to disprove the scientific theory under study, the contemporary science studies "accountant" usually approaches a scientific controversy by describing both sides in terms of, for example, social circumstances, institutional authority, and rhetorical networks.

These brief, introductory remarks highlight the differences (between science studies and law/science relations) that make interdisciplinary engagement uncertain. In a trial, if litigating parties offer opposing scientific "knowledges" (or theories, or explanations), one may be deemed invalid and inadmissible; if both are admissible, the judge or jury can select the best. At that point, even if there was time for a careful analysis of the social, institutional, and rhetorical aspects of each side, no one is interested in demonstrating that both sides are correct or accurate given their respective pragmatic contexts. Indeed, each side's lawyer, during cross-examination, wants to suggest that the other side's experts are biased due to economic interests, that their testimony is based only on institutional authority and not on scientific methodology, or that their persuasiveness is mere rhetoric. The unwelcome insight for lawyers from science studies is that *all* science is inevitably interested, authoritative, and rhetorical—even the science of their own discipline. Given that those who work in science studies and in law have such different habits of thought, we rather doubt that a mutually profitable commerce of ideas will spring up anytime soon, which is too bad; if each side took a deeper look at what the other was doing, each would find something worth knowing, even though they would disagree on much.

ETHNOGRAPHY REVISITED

We are not arguing that somatostatin does not exist, nor that it does not work, but that it cannot jump out of the very network of social practice which makes possible its existence.[10]

Because contemporary science studies is commonly associated with naive social constructivism, those who study the social, institutional, and rhetorical aspects of science often go to great pains to explain what they are *not* saying. Unfortunately, it is not always clear what is being said and what is not being said; scholarly prose is seldom transparent. Even a passage like the one from Latour and Woolgar that we have just quoted can be misread, although its clarity is well above average. Consider the phrase, "which makes possible its existence." If one focuses on identification of the hormone itself, the passage states what is true: the discovery (over thirty years ago) of somatostatin, as well as the manufacture, distribution, prescription, and consumption of a drug that mimics somatostatin, were made possible only by a "network of social practice." However, if one were to focus on the biology and chemistry of the hormone, the passage is profoundly misleading. Social practice made possible our knowledge of the biochemistry of the hormone, but it did not call this biochemistry into existence. We fear that in reading Latour and Woolgar, the reader must distinguish epistemology from ontology more carefully than the authors do.

Alan Gross, famous for his claim that "scientific knowledge is not special, but social; the result not of revelations, but of persuasion," ends his fascinating study of the inevitable, constitutive role of rhetoric in science with an epilogue on the realism debate:

> Those who resist the notion that science is fundamentally rhetorical point to the "brute facts": planes fly, men cannot have babies . . . . But a rhetoric of science denies none of these . . . . The claim of rhetoric is that the phrase "brute facts" is an oxymoron. Facts are by nature linguistic—no language, no facts.[11]

While Gross's rhetoric about rhetoric is clever, it does not persuade us, because it lumps what should be split. In the above passage, Gross fails to distinguish a concept's content from its reference. Consider the phrase "no language, no facts." It is true that facts are expressed in language; it is also true that the word *fact* has a linguistic meaning—this meaning gets its rhetorical force from its opposition to other concepts such as fiction or theory. However, when one states facts, one attempts to refer, and sometimes succeeds, to that which is nonlinguistic. In sum, Gross's claim that science is "fundamentally rhetorical" will be rejected by anyone who believes that science is fundamentally referential. Gross's bad rhetoric is unfortunate, since his book as a whole has merit.

Barry Barnes, associated with the "strong programme" social constructivism that has been accused of replacing nature with society (or social interests) as the determinant of scientific knowledge, rejects the view

> that reality has nothing to do with what we say of it. Nor does it follow [from the view that reality will tolerate alternative descriptions] that because language is not constrained and fixed by what it is used to refer to, it has no referential aspect at all. Uncritical acceptance of assumptions of this kind represents an overreaction to realism.[12]

Barnes is rightly concerned that when sociologists of knowledge claim "that [scientists] treat their own knowledge as valid only in certain circumstances or under certain conditions," this is often misread as a claim "that [scientists'] knowledge is not valid"—a common misconception. Such concerns point to what has been called the "naturalist turn" in science studies.[13] However Barnes, like Latour, Woolgar, and Gross, does not sufficiently emphasize the way in which the constraints of reality mix with the constraints of society. None of them give equal time to both constraints; because they are challenging the idealization of science, they devote all of their energy to describing the social aspects of science, which limits (but does not negate) the force of their arguments.

The potential of science studies to contribute to understanding the scientific enterprise, in litigation and even in policy debates, depends in part on avoiding the popular misunderstanding that science studies is in denial concerning the utility of scientific knowledge. Indeed, in the second edition of *Laboratory Life* (1986), Latour and Woolgar omitted the word *social* from their subtitle, "The [Social] Construction of Scientific Facts," in recognition that the term no longer has meaning.

"Social" retained meaning [in early sociology of science] to define a realm of study which excluded considerations of "scientific" context. It also had meaning in [strong social constructivism] to explain the technical content of science [in terms of external influence] (by contrast with internalist explanations of technical content). In all such uses, "social" was primarily a term of antagonism, one part of a binary opposition.[14]

We might say that science studies is trying to become a friendly interdiscipline, interested more in adding to our understanding of science than in seeming to claim that science bears no relation to reality.

What do studies of the social, institutional, and rhetorical aspects of science add to our practical understanding of science? From one perspective, the careful study of what scientists do, of how they speak and write, is trivial. Of course science is uncertain, changes over time, is dependent on measurement devices, requires funding, involves human beings and social institutions, relies on language and persuasion, and so forth. Latour and Woolgar note that the reaction of the Salk Institute scientists they studied was that "it was all rather unsurprising": "How could anyone *ignore* the details of our daily work?"[15] As to rhetoric, John Nelson likewise remarks that while it is easy to show that all disciplines are rhetorical, since they are "personal, institutional, and therefore political, some dismiss this as a truism that could never carry significant implications . . . . It is, they maintain, like learning that you have always spoken prose: true but with no practical consequences."[16] On the other hand, it is precisely the rhetoric of science that trivializes its social and institutional aspects, and that denies its rhetorical and narrative features.[17] Even when these social aspects of science are relatively trivial, a scrupulous description will include them. Indeed, scholars who study the rhetoric of science have shown that despite the "notion . . . that scientific discourse is . . . devoid of the rhetorical and metaphorical maneuvers that are common in" other disciplines,[18] there is no

escape from informal argumentation, or from figures or tropes, or from selective naming and framing of issues, or from appeals to commonly-held values, or from the need to adapt arguments to ends, audiences, and circumstances.[19]

Moreover, scientific discourse "is rhetorical in a constitutive rather than ornamental fashion"[20]—that is, "style is epistemic," since "rhetorical figures . . . *enable* scientists to develop and extend their knowledge about scientific concepts."[21] And yet, the rhetoric of science is hidden in a discourse that typically denies its rhetoricity. For example, the dominant style of agentless prose in scientific literature unwittingly suggests that nature is speaking, while the passive scientist merely observes and records results under the force of nature.[22]

Social and institutional aspects of science likewise are rendered invisible as contingencies, as opposed, again, to the "essentially cognitive elements which have traditionally been supposed to be solely responsible for the constitution of scientific knowledge."[23]

> The result of the *construction* of a fact is that it appears unconstructed by anyone; the result of rhetorical persuasion . . . is that participants are convinced that they have not been convinced; . . . the result of the investments of credibility, is that participants can claim that economics and belief are in no way related to the solidity of science; as to the circumstances, they simply vanish from accounts . . . .[24]

This situation leads to the conviction in science studies that sociologists cannot simply look to internalist (or "official") accounts, including the formal text of a published scientific paper, "as a reliable guide to the actions involved in producing it and to other actions on which it reports." Scientists' own accounts of their actions (e.g., theorizing and experiments) "will always look as though they were legitimately constitutive of scientific knowledge," precisely because references to personal or social contingencies are systematically eliminated in the course of formal discourse. However, in scientists' informal discussions, gossip, and humor, the "part played by social and personal contingencies in scientific action and belief" is often more obvious.[25] This is not to say that scientists acknowledge, or grant constitutive relevancy to, social and institutional determinants, but only that (perhaps indirect) *references* to contingent matters will appear more clearly in informal discourse. That is why the ethnographic interview and the practice of "following scientists around" have become methodologies in science studies.

Like the anthropologist who views culture as a "silent language" of unconscious traditions and conventions,[26] the scholar of science studies attempts to "provide insights into those aspects of [scientific] culture taken for granted by its members."[27] Just as the traditional Western ethnographer lived with and observed an alien culture,[28] the science studies scholar, using an ethnographic approach, adopts the perspective of the stranger to maintain analytic distance from the conventional "explanations of activities prevalent within the culture being observed."[29] And just as the anthropological ethnographer ideally "moves . . . from data to idea"—meanwhile remaining open to the "unanticipated realities of fieldwork," and to the possibility that a preplanned inquiry "is misleading and irrelevant"[30]—the science studies ethnographer "*does not know* the nature of the society under study, nor where to draw the boundaries between the realms of technical, social, scientific, natural, and so on."[31]

The value of the ethnographic interview is in our view not to criticize science or to challenge its successes. The sociologist or anthropologist of science, after all, is not trying to show that because a particular scientific activity is a social enterprise, it is bad science. The goal is rather to "examine how objects of knowledge are constituted in science," including the "processes of interaction between scientists and others within which and through which scientific beliefs take shape."[32] This neutrality—keeping in mind that all science is inevitably social, institutional, and rhetorical—contrasts sharply with the view that such factors signal error or deficiencies.[33] The latter view, associated with early sociology of science,[34] would likely be shared with litigators who identify (during cross-examination of experts) financial, occupational, methodological, or political interests as potential biases that interfere with good science.

When one first encounters the growth of the disciplines of science studies (including science and technology studies, the sociology of scientific knowledge, and cultural studies of science), their prominence in numerous university programs, and the appropriation of anthropological methodology in ethnographic studies of scientific practice, one cannot help but think that the insights of this field would be useful to judges and lawyers who, in cases involving scientific expertise, need to understand how science works. As has been shown, however, science studies does not fit easily into much of the discourse of law and science relations, where an idealized conception of science predominates. Interest, bias, and motivation are viewed in the courtroom as bases for impeachment or as markers of junk science, in contrast to the bases of genuine scientific knowledge: sufficient data and reliable methodology. Evidence that all science is socially motivated, institutionally interested, or rhetorically biased seems to have no place in the courtroom, since it casts doubt on the certitude of *both* sides' expertise. The value of science studies for law is therefore called into question.

On the other hand, if science studies is viewed as a challenge not to science itself but to our idealizations of science, then the appellate judges who authored the opinions discussed in chapters 2 and 3 seem to understand science in ways that overlap much of the current understanding of science in science studies. In both, one finds modest and realistic views of science. In both, one can find an emphasis on how science is actually done. And in both, the actual process of doing science is respected. Indeed, the mere fact that one can show that social factors generated a particular bit of science is no longer viewed as proof that the science so produced is impure or dubious. Social factors can be responsible for helping science be good science.

THE HISTORY OF SCIENCE: AN EXAMPLE FROM GALISON

Peter Galison's wonderful book *Einstein's Clocks, Poincaré's Maps* is a good example of how science studies should be done. He wants to explain a change, and so he begins his book with a statement of the *status quo ante*; he begins by stating the scientific worldview that would be changed by Einstein's revolution: "True time would never be revealed by mere clocks—of this Newton was sure."[35] As most know, in Einstein's world, clocks are not "mere clocks" anymore; after Einstein has worked his revolution, clocks will define time, and *time* will have no meaning other than that which is measured by suitably synchronized clocks.

Galison's project is to explain how we got to the new world that Einstein's name has come to symbolize, and so he states a misconception that he wishes to challenge. Einstein presented his new view (which eventually became the standard position held by all physicists) in his famous 1905 paper on special relativity. Galison notes a common impression that many hold about this famous paper: "Einstein's argument, as usually understood, departs so radically from the older, 'practical' world of classical mechanics that the paper has become a model of revolutionary thought, seen as fundamentally detached from a material, intuitive relation to the world."[36] Galison's thesis is that Einstein was not detached from the world; indeed, the problem that he attacked was part of the common intellectual and practical agenda of engineers, scientists, surveyors, cartographers, railroad companies, and telegraph companies of the time. (In what follows, we shall neglect entirely Galison's discussions of Poincaré's role in the great revolution of our understanding of time; Poincaré played a major role in the historical story, but we do not have space to do him justice.)

Galison's project of re-embedding Einstein in a social context is a model that we wish to cite. (We are not so presumptuous as to claim that our text gives authority to Galison's; rather, it is the other way around.) Our thesis in this book has been that science is a communal activity and that the social context within which a scientist works can help generate good science. We have tried to avoid the simplicity of saying that the social context produces science, which would entail that science is purely a social construction. We have also tried to avoid the simplification that scientific methodology produces science, which would entail that science is independent of the social world. The chief difficulty is stating the middle ground, but happily enough, Galison's book helps us understand what the middle ground looks like.

The first way in which Galison helps is by telling a richly detailed story about the social contexts in which many before Einstein were grappling with problems of time. The railroads were strong supporters of synchronizing clocks since the safety and the efficiency of railroad operations depended on coordinating their schedules.[37] Cartographers also needed to have an accurate determination of time in order to calculate longitude, and so synchronizing clocks that were far distant from each other was an intensely practical problem for them.[38] As the demand for accuracy increased, the simple solution of carrying a chronometer set to home time and comparing that chronometer to local noon no longer sufficed. And so the telegraph, and then the radio, was used to send a time signal over long distances.[39] However, if one sends a time signal over a long distance, then one must also know something about how long it takes the signal to make its journey.

Determining the transmission time of a signal was not only a practical question for cartographers; it was also one of the key moves in Einstein's theoretical achievement. To show the link between cartography and Einstein's relativity, let us quote the second paragraph in Galison's book:

> At the heart of [Einstein's rejection of Newton's concept of absolute time] . . . lay an extraordinary yet easily stated idea that has remained dead-center in physics, philosophy, and technology ever since: *To talk about time, about simultaneity at a distance, you have to synchronize two clocks, you have to start with one, flash a signal to the other, and adjust for the time that the flash takes to arrive.* What could be simpler? Yet with this procedural definition of time, the last piece of the relativity puzzle fell into place, changing physics forever.[40]

Einstein did not invent this procedure. As Galison points out, surveyors and cartographers were using this procedure as a piece of commonplace technology;[41] Poincaré had written philosophical and technical papers on this procedure;[42] and Einstein's scientific contemporaries understood his conception of time by way of their prior understanding of this technical practice.[43] In short, when Einstein presented his new theory of time to the world, he presented it to a world that was ready to receive it, to a world that was already using his definition for practical purposes but had not yet understood the implications of their practice. (Einstein's originality was not in inventing a new procedure; his originality was in putting this simple idea at the very center of a theory of physics and in using this idea to spin out logical consequences that no one else had anticipated.)

Furthermore, Einstein was not removed from this practical world. He did not observe the world from an ivory tower; his work in the Swiss patent office put him in the midst of the practical world. Even before he went to the patent office, he had done considerable experimental work in thermodynamics and electrodynamics at a first-rate technical university.[44] The patent office was itself a first-rate educational institution. Einstein's supervisor, Friedrich Haller, was a stern taskmaster who demanded that Einstein add skills in technical drawing and machine technology to his obvious skills in physics, and when Einstein succeeded in meeting these demands, he was duly promoted.[45] Furthermore, the intellectual task of a patent examiner fitted well with Einstein's iconoclastic mind. Haller demanded that his subordinates be critical and skeptical, and that they test every assumption and assertion of a patent application.[46] Not only did Einstein's work in the patent office put him in touch with developments in the technology of time synchronization, it probably had some influence on the style in which he wrote the famous 1905 paper on special relativity. As Galison notes, this famous paper "does not . . . look like an ordinary physics paper," insofar as it has hardly any footnotes to other authors, only a few equations, no discussion of experimental results, and so forth.[47] However, the style of the paper does resemble the style of a patent claim, and so Galison suggests Einstein's patent office experience as the most obvious source for what seems like a stylistic quirk.[48] Indeed, Einstein later remarked in a letter to a friend that his stylistic preference for clarity and concreteness was shaped by his experience in the patent office.[49] And finally, perhaps it is worth noting that Einstein genuinely enjoyed his work in the patent office. The romantic temptation to imagine that Einstein was forced to do drudge work is contradicted by his own testimony: "Working on the final formulation of technological patents was a veritable blessing for me. It enforced many-sided thinking and also provided important stimuli to physical thought."[50]

The business of the patent office in the relevant years (from 1902 when Einstein began to work there to 1905 when he published the famous paper) fit the topic of special relativity quite nicely. Numerous patents dealt with clocks and time. There were patents for using clocks to activate remote alarms, to monitor railroad departures and arrivals, and to send time signals by telephone or wirelessly.[51] Indeed, some of the patents dealt specifically, and not merely by inference, with proposals to set simultaneous times for remote clocks.[52] Given that Einstein's job responsibilities included this type of device, the inference is irresistible that he must have worked on these patents, approving some and rejecting others. Unfortunately, we must rest content with reasonable inference; as Galison notes: "Sadly, the Swiss patent office dutifully destroyed all papers processed by Einstein eighteen years after their creation; this was standard procedure on patent opinions, and even Einstein's fame led to no exception."[53] (That we must rest on an inference without perfect evidence is the thesis of our book, and we note that Galison did not refrain from inference merely because his evidence was not perfect.)

Once we see that the relationship of Einstein's science to the technology of his day was far richer than we had imagined before reading Galison's book, then a rather obvious question must be asked: What were the historical dynamics? That is, what sort of link might there be between the social context and the scientific theory? This link is the theme of Galison's book, and in the book he distinguishes his way of understanding the link from two of the common ways that stories such as this one are told.

> In telling of the relation between the pure and applied, there are narratives that track abstract ideas down through laboratories to the machine-shop floor and into everyday life. There are also stories that run the other way, in which the daily workings of technology are slowly refined as they shed their materiality on the way up the ladder of abstraction until they reach theory—from the shop floor to the laboratory to the blackboard, and eventually to the arcane reaches of philosophy. Indeed, science often does function this way: from the purity of an ethereal vapor, ideas may seem to condense into everyday matter; conversely, ideas seem to sublime from the solid, quotidian world into air.[54]

Since Galison believes that neither of these two metaphors (from cloud to ground or ground to cloud) will work, however, he substitutes an extravagant metaphor of his own, which we shall quote in full.

> Imagine an ocean covered by a confined atmosphere of water vapor. When this world is hot enough, the water evaporates; when the water cools, it condenses and rains down into the ocean. But if the pressure and heat are such that, as the water expands, the vapor is compressed, eventually the liquid and the gas approach the same density. As that critical point nears, something quite extraordinary occurs. Water and vapor no longer remain stable; instead, all through this world, pockets of liquid and vapor begin to flash back and forth between the two phases, from vapor to liquid, from liquid to vapor—from tiny clusters of molecules to volumes nearly the size of the planet. At this critical point, light of different wavelengths begins reflecting off drops of different sizes—purple off smaller drops, red off larger ones. Soon, light is bouncing off at every possible wavelength. Every color of the visible spectrum is reflected as if from mother-of-pearl. Such wildly fluctuating phase changes reflect light with what is known as critical opalescence.
>
> This is the metaphor we need for coordinated time. Once in a great while a scientific-technological shift occurs that cannot be understood in the cleanly separated domains of technology, science, or philosophy. The coordination of time in the half-century following 1860 does not sublime in a slow, even-paced process from the technological field upward into the more rarified realms of science and philosophy. Nor did ideas of time synchronization originate in a pure realm of thought and then condense into the objects and actions of machines and factories. In its fluctuations back and forth between the abstract and the concrete,

in its variegated scales, time coordination emerges in the volatile phase changes of critical opalescence.[55]

In this book, we do not speak of the sort of epochal scientific change that Galison addresses; we wish to understand the best ways to present science in a courtroom. Although our topic is pedestrian, it is also messy, as are most things connected with trials, which are places where greed and passion intersect with lofty principles of justice. In our lawyers' world, Galison's metaphor of the chaotic phase changes of critical opalescence seems apt; his metaphor seems to fit better than the metaphors of evaporation or condensation. Furthermore, his metaphor seems to have more than mere descriptive power; it seems to have normative power. We think it wrong to demand that the science used at law be either the straightforward condensation of theory into testimony or the simple sublimation of facts into theory. Our normative principles must be more complex than that given by such simple pictures.

THE POLICY CONTEXT: THE EXAMPLE OF TENNCARE

Having presented a happy picture, we now turn to a sad one. Galison is a model of how one should think about the interplay between science and society; the TennCare legislation we shall discuss is the exact opposite. But what is TennCare?[56] It is the Tennessee version of Medicaid. (States are encouraged under national law to devise plans for providing health care; if the secretary of Health and Human Services approves a state plan, then the state can substitute their program for the national program that would otherwise be in place.) Like all health care programs, whether public or private, the TennCare program provides services if the services are "medically necessary."

Although the concept of medical necessity is absolutely crucial in the field of health care, it can be variously defined, and whatever the definition, it can be variously administered.[57] And I suppose that we will not shock anyone if we state that politicians have attempted to manipulate this definition for political purposes.[58] The political purpose in Tennessee was to deal with a budget crunch. The legislative solution was to adopt a new definition of medical necessity.[59]

We will not do a thorough analysis of the recent legislation that governs TennCare; we will focus solely on two provisions of that legislation that are examples of using an idealized view of science as a smokescreen for rationing medical care. The first is a provision that requires any "medical item or service" to be "safe and effective." The definition of this concept reads as follows:

To qualify as safe and effective, the type and level of medical item or service must be consistent with the symptoms or diagnosis and treatment of the particular medical condition, and the reasonably anticipated medical benefits of the item or service must outweigh the reasonably anticipated medical risks based on the enrollee's condition and scientifically supported evidence.[60]

There are several idealizations in this provision, although on first reading these provisions seem both innocent and obviously valid. Consider the requirement that the medical benefits must outweigh the medical risks. Who could object to this? Surely benefits should be "reasonably anticipated" to exceed risks? Yet there are several issues that are concealed in this command. Who is to do the balancing? How is it to be done? For example, merely doing something so that uncertainty could be resolved might count as a benefit to some patients, but not to others, yet the rule does not suggest approval of this sort of subjectivity. Notice that the rule assumes that the calculus of balancing must be governed by "scientifically supported evidence," which suggests that the balancing must be objective. However, most students of risk assessment acknowledge that this process must be subjective if it is to be rational.[61] We agree one should use "scientifically supported evidence" if it is available, but it seems irrational to say that one is forbidden from using a calculus of balancing if such evidence is absent (as it often is), and it also seems irrational to ignore the fact that balancing risks against benefits will include both objective and subjective factors.

The subjectivity of risk assessment is perhaps best illustrated by an everyday example that is far removed from medical practice. Consider the millions of people who drive to work every day or take an airplane to go on vacation. For most of them, when the risks of travel become too high, they will not make the trip and will choose to forgo work or vacation. But few would set the level of risk at the same point for both, and they are not being irrational when they are willing to run greater risks in going to work than in going on a vacation. For both trips, there is a risk of routine mechanical failure leading to a fatal injury, but most of us hold the airlines to a higher standard than we hold our own automobiles. For both trips, we run the risk of terrorists striking, but we worry more about the terrorists who strike airplanes than about those who attack automobiles. For both trips, those who operate the autos and planes with which we share the highways and air space could lose control and kill us along with themselves, but we do not assess the risks by the same standards. There is nothing irrational about our differential standards. After all, we cannot easily forgo working, but a vacation is easy to postpone, so there is no reason to run the same risks in both.

The obvious question is "Why should we idealize science and risk taking in medicine when we do not idealize science and risk taking in transportation?" Our thesis, as should be obvious, is that we should not, and so the next provision that we quote strikes us as grossly inappropriate. This provision states that a medical procedure does not qualify under TennCare if it is "experimental or investigational." The command that one should not experiment on patients in the TennCare system might be controversial, but we can understand that reasonable minds can differ, and we also understand that those who operate a medical insurance program that is under severe budgetary distress might reasonably conclude that they must forgo the luxury of paying for experiments. However, it does not follow from these concessions that we also concede that every possible definition of "experimental or investigational" is appropriate. The following definition seems to us to be wildly off the mark.

> A medical item or service is experimental or investigational if there is inadequate empirically-based objective clinical scientific evidence of its safety and effectiveness for the particular use in question. This standard is not satisfied by a provider's subjective clinical judgment on the safety and effectiveness of a medical item or service or by a reasonable medical or clinical hypothesis based on an extrapolation from use in another setting or from use in diagnosing or treating another condition.[62]

The phrase "empirically-based objective clinical scientific evidence" is a mouthful, and it wraps up together in a single package a wide range of requirements. As we understand it, a drug would not qualify for reimbursement under TennCare unless a classic double-blind test with patients had been performed (which TennCare would not pay for). The requirement that the "scientific evidence" be "clinical" would seem to rule out the possibility of treating patients under TennCare on the basis of laboratory, epidemiological, or structural analysis.

Furthermore, one could interpret this provision to say that a classic double-blind test is only necessary, not sufficient. Note that the provision prohibits extrapolation. However, individual responses to drugs are notoriously variable. It is well known that gender, age, and race can generate variable responses, and so it might follow from the provision we quote that a double-blind test would have to be made on each possible demographic group (or the patient's particular demographic group) before one could expect reimbursement under TennCare. Furthermore, demographic variability is not the only medically relevant variable. The medical history of an individual patient and that patient's family may lead competent physicians to agree among themselves that they should prescribe a different course of drugs than they would to another patient in the same demographic group. In short, what the provision calls "extrapolation for use in another setting or from use in diagnosing or treating another condition" is fundamental to the practice of medicine, and so the provision could easily be interpreted to make medicine as we know it non-reimbursable. If so, then we are willing to confidently predict (without the benefit of scientific evidence) that the political fallout from these new TennCare provisions will be more than the politicians of Tennessee can handle, and that they will amend the recent legislation. But even if we are wrong in our political prediction (we have no record of being seers), we believe the provisions are bad on their merits. In this context, as in others, idealizing science is a bad idea.

We hope that our discussion of recent trends in science studies, of Galison's book (which describes a good example that should be emulated), and of TennCare (as a bad example that should be condemned) will be sympathetically received by scholars who puzzle over the connections between science, history, and policy. If so, then our thesis that what is happening in the courts has its parallels elsewhere should also strike a harmonious chord.

CONCLUSION

In the litigation context, the idealization of law is exemplified by Professor Robert Bohrer's explanation of the fundamental differences between science and law:

> [Science] is digital, replicable/general, and objective/universal; law is analogical, unpredictable/particular, and normative/contingent . . . .
> . . . Digital is used here to indicate that scientific research is generally intended to examine variables that are discrete, well understood, and have quantitative attributes . . . . [B]ut law is analogical[;] variables . . . . such as "negligence" . . . are "soft" conceptual categories that have no fixed boundaries and need reinterpretation . . . .
> . . . [S]cience is only science if it is predictable . . . . Law, on the other hand, . . . is particular and of very limited predictability . . . .
> . . . Science aims . . . at discovering and applying categories that are objectively derived, and which . . . permit . . . prediction universally . . . . By contrast, law is inherently normative . . . .[63]

Such statements ignore and eclipse consideration of the pragmatic aspects of science, including scientific controversies, scientific revolutions, the probabilistic nature of science, the social and institutional context of scientific practice, and the role of analogy and interpretation in science. Indeed, some legal commentators, particularly those who are oriented toward injured plaintiffs and against corporate defendants, see the potential for misuse of such a lofty picture of science.

> Scientists love to keep questioning things, and that inquisitiveness makes judges nervous. "You can manufacture uncertainty because scientists don't always agree . . . [Defense lawyers] take differences among scientists and magnify them, and as long as there is any sort of disagreement the case does not move forward."[64]

Judges, some say, display "a woeful ignorance of scientific uncertainty," and buy into the so-called sound science movement:

> "Sound science" is shorthand for a narrow definition of what counts as scientific evidence . . . . For example, it would rely on epidemiology (the study of cause and distribution of disease in populations) and would dismiss animal studies . . . .
> . . . [T]his narrow definition . . . leaves out vast areas of scientific knowledge and inquiry and many legitimate tools of investigation. Scientists themselves rely on animal studies, models, systematic field observation, and even casual observations . . . .[65]

Hence the concern that *Daubert* gatekeeping often functions to exclude legitimate scientific research.

The concern over using "sound science" as a criterion reverberates in the policy arena, where liberals accuse conservatives of using high standards to challenge, for example, environmental regulations:

> This may seem innocuous, but scientists [view conservative "sound science" legislation] as a stealthy attempt to ban one of the most reliable techniques they have for understanding the vulnerability of species: population modeling, which projects current data into the future and is thus neither exclusively empirical nor field-tested (though the initial data has to come from the field). "When [conservatives] start saying, 'you've got to give preference just to "field-tested," "peer reviewed,"' that is a total misrepresentation of how science goes," said [biologist] Gordon Orians . . . . "If you're going to say, 'we can't use models,' you might as well shut down the scientific enterprise" . . . .[66]

Just as the TennCare example shows idealization of science in the policy arena, Orians's warning demonstrates the need for a non-romantic understanding of science by lawmakers and government administrators.

To our eyes, what has happened in our nation's courts is a fine demonstration of the dangers of idealizing science and of the highly practical attempts of judges who sit on the courts of appeals to avoid false idealizations. In this chapter and book, we have tried to show that the same pitfalls and the same remedies are present in both history and public policy.

In courts, in history, and in public policy, sometimes the problems are the same and so are the solutions.

NOTES

1. Bruno Latour and Steve Woolgar, *Laboratory Life: The Construction of Scientific Facts* 69–70 (1986).

2. *See* Paul Atkinson and Martyn Hammersly, "Ethnography and Participant Observation," in *Strategies of Qualitative Inquiry* (ed. Norman K. Denzin and Yvonna S. Lincoln, 1998), at 113.

3. *See generally* Latour and Woolgar, *supra* note 1.

The approach chosen by Bruno Latour was to become part of a laboratory, to follow closely the daily and intimate processes of scientific work, while at the same time to remain an "inside" outside observer, a kind of anthropological probe to study a scientific "culture"—to follow in every detail what the scientists do and how and what they think.

Jonas Salk, "Introduction," in *id.* at 12.

4. *See* David Faigman, David Kaye, Michael Saks, and Joseph Sanders, *Science in the Law: Social and Behavioral Science Issues* viii (2002).

5. *See id.* at v, citing John Brockman, *The Third Culture* (1995) (emergence of a "third culture" through an increasing number of scientists writing for a general audience).

6. *See, e.g.*, Michael Mulkay, Jonathan Potter, and Steven Yearley, "Why an Analysis of Scientific Discourse is Needed," in *Science Observed: Perspectives on the Social Study of Science* (ed. Karin D. Knorr-Cetina and Michael Mulkay, 1983). In formal literature, scientists

rely almost exclusively on what has been called an empiricist repertoire. Stylistically, this means that scientists write in a conventionally impersonal manner. By reducing explicit references to human agency to a minimum, authors construct texts in which the physical world often seems literally to speak and act for itself. When the author is allowed to appear in the text, he is presented either as being forced . . . to reach theoretical conclusions . . . by the unequivocal demands of the natural phenomena which he is studying or as being rigidly constrained by rules of experimental procedure.

Id. at 197. Criteria such as testability are often "presented as constituting a clear-cut, impersonal, unavoidable constraint on the choice of correct theories." *See id.* at 198. In such accounts, scientific theorizing, experiments, and corresponding publications and criticism in learned journals are constitutive, being "essentially cognitive elements which have traditionally been supposed to be solely responsible for the constitution of scientific knowledge." *See id.* at 183. Compare *Daubert*, 509 U.S. at 593–94 (valid science usually involves testability, low error rate, peer-reviewed publication, and general acceptance).

7. *See generally* Latour and Woolgar, *supra* note 1.

8. *See generally* Paul Gross and Norman Levitt, *Higher Superstitions: The Academic Left and Its Quarrels with Science* (1994).

9. *See* Mulkay et al., *supra* note 6, at 198–99 (criticizing the "regular pattern of accounting" in internal scientific accounts, and recommending discourse analysis which would be "rather like a natural history of social accounting").

10. Latour and Woolgar, *supra* note 1, at 183.

11. *See* Alan G. Gross, *The Rhetoric of Science* 20, 202–3 (1990).

12. *See* Barry Barnes, "How Not to Do the Sociology of Knowledge," in *Rethinking Objectivity* (ed. Allan Megill, 1994), at 31–32.

13. *See generally* Werner Callebaut, *Taking the Naturalist Turn, or, How Real Philosophy of Science Is Done* (1993); *see also* David S. Caudill, "Law and Science: An Essay on Links and Socio-Natural Hybrids," 51 *Syracuse L. Rev.* 841, 853–61 (2001) (discussing various accommodations of reality or nature in recent science studies, such as constrained constructivism and agential realism).

14. *See* Latour and Woolgar, *supra* note 1, at 281 (postscript to second edition).

15. *See* Latour and Woolgar, *supra* note 1, at 274.

16. *See* John S. Nelson, *Tropes of Politics: Science, Theory, Rhetoric, Action* 47 (1998).

17. *See* Gross, *supra* note 11, at 32 ("for scientists, the results of science depend not on argument but on nature herself").

18. *See* Richard D. Johnson-Sheehan, "Metaphor in the Rhetoric of Scientific Discourse," in *Essays in the Study of Scientific Discourse: Methods, Practice, and Pedagogy* (ed. John Battalio, 1998), at 167.

19. *See* Herbert W. Simons, "The Rhetoric of the Scientific Research Report: 'Drug-pushing' in a Medical Journal Article," in *The Recovery of Rhetoric: Persuasive Discourse and Disciplinarity in the Human Sciences* (ed. R. H. Roberts and J. J. M. Good, 1993), at 150.

20. *See* Gay M. Gragson and Ted L. Gragson, "Uncertain Science and the Sponsored-Research Process," in *Essays in the Study of Scientific Discourse*, *supra* note 18, at 19 ("Scientific claims are accepted only if they persuade the community within which they are put forward").

21. *See* Heather Brodie Graves, "Marbles, Dimples, Rubber Sheets, and Quantum Wells: The Role of Analogy in the Rhetoric of Science," 28 *Rhetoric Society Q.* 25, 26, 45 (1998).

22. *See* David Locke, "Voices of Science," 67 *Am. Scholar* 103, 104 (1998) (the official language of science "is what English teachers call agentless prose").

23. *See* Mulkay et al., *supra* note 6, at 183.

24. *See* Latour and Woolgar, *supra* note 1, at 240.

25. *See* Mulkay et al., *supra* note 6, at 178, 191–97.

26. *See* James L. Peacock, *The Anthropological Lens: Harsh Light, Soft Focus* 4 (1986); *see also* Richard A. Barrett, *Culture and Conduct: An Excursion in Anthropology* 54–55 (1984).

27. *See* Latour and Woolgar, *supra* note 1, at 278.

28. *See* Peacock, *supra* note 26, at 18–19 (ethnography, "the most distinctive kind of anthropological research," means "a description of a certain way of life," based on fieldwork, that is, "living with and observing a living group").

29. *See* Latour and Woolgar, *supra* note 1, at 278. "It is not necessary to travel to foreign countries to obtain this effect, even though this is the only way that many anthropologists have been able to achieve 'distance.'" *Id.* at 279.

30. *See* Peacock, *supra* note 26, at 69. ("In short, research in fieldwork often begins with encounter, then proceeds to interpretation").

31. *See* Latour and Woolgar, *supra* note 1, at 279.

32. *See* Karin D. Knorr-Cetina, "The Ethnographic Study of Scientific Work: Toward a Constructivist Interpretation of Science," in *Science Observed, supra* note 6, at 115–17.

33. *See* Latour and Woolgar, *supra* note 1, at 23 (emphasis "on 'social' in contradistinction to 'technical' can lead to the disproportionate selection of events for analysis which appear to exemplify 'mistaken' or 'wrong' science").

34. *See* Jonathan Potter, *Representing Reality: Discourse, Rhetoric, and Social Construction* 17–18 (1996).

35. Peter Galison, *Einstein's Clocks, Poincaré's Maps* 13 (2003).

36. *Id.* at 14.

37. *See, e.g., id.* at 30 (topic of railroads is introduced); 98–100 (railroad crashes caused by lack of uniformity in time); 122–28 (railroads support uniform time zones); 156–58 (Von Moltke argues that military efficiency depends on coordinated time).

38. *See id.* at 101–4 (Europeans note American achievements); 174–98 (French efforts to determine longitude linked to French national pride and the needs of empire).

39. For an account of the Eiffel Tower's place in radio time, *see id.* at 275–82.

40. *Id.* at 14–15 (emphasis in original).

41. *Id.* at 183–86.

42. *Id.* at 187–90, 277–78.

43. *Id.* at 282–85.

44. *Id.* at 228–31.

45. *Id.* at 243–46.

46. *Id.* at 243.

47. *See id.* at 290.

48. *See id.* at 291–92.

49. *See id.* at 251.

50. *Id.* at 241.

51. *Id.* at 246–47.

52. *Id.* at 247–48.

53. *Id.* at 347 n.54.

54. *Id.* at 39. Both of these alternatives have been used for the narrative frame in understanding Einstein; *see id.* at 323–24.

55. *Id.* at 39–40.

56. *See* H.B. 3513 (Tennessee 2004) (proposed amendment to the TennCare Demonstration Project).

57. For information about litigation of this concept, the interested reader can consult the website of the National Health Law Program, www.healthlaw.org

58. We are unable to resist the temptation to quote from the film *Casablanca*: "I'm shocked, shocked, to find that gambling is going on in here." And it also appears that there is politics in health care.

59. We learned about the new rules for TennCare from Professor Sara Rosenbaum, chair of the Department of Health Policy, George Washington University School of Public Health and Health Services, when she made a presentation at a faculty colloquium at Washington and Lee University School of Law.

60. Refer to note 56 *supra*.

61. *See generally*, Cary Coglianese and Gary Marchant, "Shifting Sands: The Limits of Science in Setting Rule Standards," 152 *U. Pa. L. Rev.* 1255, 1257–58 ("even though science is valuable for what it can tell administrators about policy problems and their possible solutions, science alone cannot provide a complete rationale for a policy decision because it does not address the normative aspects of administrative policymaking"); M. Granger Morgan, "Risk Analysis and Management," *Sci. Am.*, July 1993, at 32 ("Laypeople have different, broader definitions of risk, which in important respects can be more rational than the narrow ones used by experts").

62. *See* H.B. 3513 (Tennessee 2004).

63. Robert A. Bohrer, "The Fundamental Differences between Science and Law," in *Expert Witnessing: Explaining and Understanding Science* (ed. Carl Meyer, 1999), at 41–43.

64. Peg Brickley, "Science v. Law: A Decade-Old Rule on Scientific Evidence Comes under Fire," *Sci. Am.*, Dec. 2003, at 32.

65. Carolyn Raffensperger, "Detox for Torts (Part I)," *The Networker*, Science and Environmental Health Network, June 2003, at www.sehn.org/Volume_8-3.html.

66. Chris Mooney, "Sucker Punch: How Conservatives Are Trying to Use a Conflict over Obscure Fish to Gut the Science behind the Endangered Species Act," *Legal Affairs*, May/June 2004, at 24.

Index

Page listings that appear in italics refer to figures on that page.

About the Authors

David S. Caudill is a professor of law and the Arthur M. Goldberg Family Chair in Law at Villanova University School of Law. He is author of *Disclosing Tilt: Law, Belief, and Criticism* (1989), *Lacan and the Subject of Law: Toward a Psychoanalytic Critical Legal Theory* (1994), and *Property: Cases, Documents, and Lawyering Strategies* (2004).

Lewis H. LaRue is a professor of law and Class of 1958 Alumni Professor of Law Emeritus at Washington and Lee University School of Law. He is author of *Political Discourse: A Case Study of the Watergate Affair* (1988) and *Constitutional Law as Fiction: Narrative in the Rhetoric of Authority* (1995).

CPSIA information can be obtained at www.ICGtesting.com
Printed in the USA
LVOW092326220112

265079LV00005B/119/P